An introduction to
Transformational Education

A Theoretical Model for Driving Student Success

An Introduction to TRANSFORMATIONAL EDUCATION
Redefining Leadership in the Classroom

GT FREEMAN

ꞵ FlutterBy Press

This book presents stories and testimonials, with some names and details changed, events shortened, and dialogue adapted for clarity.

Copyright © 2025 by The Lincoln Center for Family and Youth

All rights reserved.
No part of this publication may be reproduced, stored in a retrieval system, or transmitted in any form or by any means electronic, mechanical, photocopying, recording or otherwise, without the prior written permission of the publisher.

Published by
FlutterBy Press | www.flutterbypress.com

Publisher's Cataloging-in-Publication Data
Freeman, G.T.

An introduction to transformational education : redefining leadership in the classroom / G.T. Freeman. – Audubon, PA : FlutterBy Press, 2025.

p. ; cm.

ISBN13: 978-0-9601259-0-6

1. Educational change. 2. Educational leadership
3. Learning. 4. Educational innovations. I. Title.
II. Freeman, G.T.

LB2806 .F74 2024
371.2--dc23

Project Coordination
Jenkins Group, Inc. | www.jenkinsgroupinc.com

Design Credits
Cover design: Yvonne Fetig Roehler
Interior design: Brooke Camfield

Printing
Printed in the United States of America
29 28 27 26 25 • 5 4 3 2 1

Dedication

Dedicated to Gary L. Grenier (1948–2023), whose visionary leadership as former CEO indelibly shaped The Lincoln Center for Family and Youth. Through his unwavering commitment to Transformational Education, he not only inspired this book but also left an enduring impact on the institution he deeply cherished.

"If I have seen further, it is by standing on the shoulders of giants."

—Sir Isaac Newton

Contents

Acknowledgments	ix
About the Author	xi
About The Lincoln Center for Family and Youth	xiii
Preface	xv
Introduction to Transformational Education	3

Chapter 1
Teacher Behaviors | The Origin of the Ripple — 15

   1.1 Authentic Engagement — 19

   1.2 Meaning Making — 22

   1.3 Personalized Support — 30

   1.4 Stimulating Curiosity — 40

Chapter 2
School Climate | The Optimal Environment — 45

   2.1 Classroom Support — 48

   2.2 School Kindness — 53

   2.3 Aesthetic Guidance — 57

Chapter 3
Student Wellness | The First Ripples　　63

   3.1 Connectedness　　64

   3.2 Self-Efficacy　　69

   3.3 Socio-Emotional Well-Being　　76

Chapter 4
Student Performance | The Wave　　83

   4.1 Engagement　　84

   4.2 Academic Performance　　88

   4.3 Prosocial Behaviors　　91

Summary and Call to Action　　99

Appendix A | Glossary of Terms　　103

Appendix B | Endnotes　　107

Acknowledgments

For their leadership and support of The Lincoln Center (TLC), my sincerest gratitude is extended to TLC's Board of Directors: Scott Patrohay (Chair), Dr. Donna Sarhaan (Vice Chair), Henrietta Heisler, Bob Holland, Kelley Tate, Dodie Williams, and Kirk Wycoff.

For their part in codifying the Transformational Education model, I thank Dr. MaryJo Burchard, Jay Blackstone, and Cathrin Myburgh. For their contributions to this book and for making each workday fun and productive, I thank my TLC colleagues: Kerri Blakey, Rob D'Alonzo, Sara Dryka, Emily Gatto, Meghan Keaveny, Michael Quintiliano, and April Thomas.

I offer my deepest thanks to writer-editor Amy Lynch for her support, insight, and expertise. Her guidance has been instrumental in bringing this project to life. Quite simply, this book would not have happened without Amy's assistance.

Finally, I thank my wife, Heather, and my adult children—Brienna, Lauren, and Holly—for their love, sacrifice, and patience throughout my decades-long educational journey. Their constant support has been my foundation every step of the way. I'm grateful to my parents, Tommy and Jolene, for their support over the years, and to my brother, Dwain, for modeling how to successfully integrate personal passion with vocation.

—GT Freeman

About the Author

Dr. GT Freeman is the president and CEO of The Lincoln Center for Family and Youth, a social enterprise focused on empowering minds and transforming lives through mental and behavioral health counseling, alternative youth education, wellness coaching, and trauma-informed professional development. The agency also offers grant-writing services to school districts, universities, hospitals, and nonprofit organizations.

With over 30 years of leadership experience in Fortune 100 corporations, small businesses, and nonprofits, GT has served in roles such as executive education program director at North Carolina State University, senior evaluator for US Department of Education grants, and administrator of a K–12 private school. Earlier in his career, he held senior leadership positions in the technology and financial services industries.

GT holds a bachelor's degree in mechanical engineering from NC State, an MBA from UNC–Chapel Hill, and a PhD in organizational leadership from Regent University. He is a Certified Fund Raising Executive, Board Certified Coach, and Lean Six Sigma Black Belt.

GT and his wife, Heather, have three adult daughters and two grandchildren. He enjoys spending time with family, traveling, and serving in his church.

About The Lincoln Center for Family and Youth

The Lincoln Center (TLC), founded in 1970 by a behavioral health hospital and incorporated in 1983 as a 501(c)(3) nonprofit, is an entrepreneurial social enterprise dedicated to transforming lives and communities—one moment, one choice, one connection at a time. Headquartered in Philadelphia, TLC extends its reach across multiple states providing K–12 alternative education, comprehensive mental and behavioral health counseling, wellness coaching, and trauma-informed training. TLC also offers grant-writing support to assist school districts, universities, hospitals, police departments, and other nonprofit agencies in securing funding.

TLC is comprised of five programs: TLC Leadership Academies, TLC Education Institute, TLC Wellness, School-Based Services, and Community-Based Services. These programs unite under TLC's mission of "empowering people to make positive choices, meaningful connections, and transformational change."

For more information about The Lincoln Center for Family and Youth, please visit TheLincolnCenter.com

Preface

Welcome to *An Introduction to Transformational Education: Redefining Leadership in the Classroom.* This book exists to redefine traditional leadership roles within the educational landscape. It is tailored for educators, parents, students, and anyone drawn to the transformative potential of learning, offering insights and guidance for all.

At its core, Transformational Education (TE) positions teachers as pivotal school leaders. The pedagogical model outlines the interplay between teacher actions, school climate, student wellness, and academic outcomes. It advocates for four key teacher behaviors: building authentic connections with students, helping learners find purpose in their studies and in life, providing customized and personalized support, and fostering a classroom culture of curiosity and exploration.

For educators, this text contains strategies to elevate teaching methodologies. The book presents a theoretical argument for the adoption of TE in schools, emphasizing the critical leadership role of teachers in influencing, inspiring, motivating, and supporting students. The companion book, *An Application Guide to Transformational Education*, serves as a practical resource for teachers, featuring lesson plans, case studies, and self-evaluation tools designed to aid in the application and mastery of transformative teaching techniques.

For parents, guardians, and students, the book offers a new lens through which to view education. The book champions a unified approach, promoting a synergy between home and educational settings to enhance student well-being and success. It calls for a collective engagement in advocating for and implementing TE practices.

Those interested in the wider impact of education on individual growth and societal advancement will find this book a compelling read. It delves into how adopting transformational practices can instigate widespread positive change, urging a reevaluation of our contributions to the educational system, whether directly involved or as proponents of significant, systemic change. To all readers: may the insights, inspiration, and practical advice contained within these pages ignite a transformative shift in your educational approach and, by extension, effect positive and meaningful transformation in lives and communities.

Transformational Education: Redefining Leadership in the Classroom

Introduction to Transformational Education

It was a routine day during the spring semester of my eighth-grade school year when I heard over the classroom intercom, "GT Freeman, please report immediately to the guidance counselor's office." Although I had been summoned to the assistant principal's office before for disciplinary reasons related to typical boyhood antics, this seemed unusual. The message repeated, "GT, please report to *Mr. Sellers's office.*" Mr. Sellers, the *guidance counselor*? Confused, I wondered what I could have done this time.

I was attending a small rural middle school in North Carolina, and it was during the time of year when eighth-grade students registered for high school classes. When the homeroom teacher passed around a list of ninth-grade courses, I signed up for the easiest, non-college-track options. Neither of my parents attended college, and there was no discussion about college at home. My father and I watched numerous UNC–Chapel Hill basketball games together, so in my naivety, I assumed college was just a place where one went to play hoops.

I sat down in one of the chairs opposite Mr. Sellers's desk. He got right to the point. In a friendly voice, he asked, "GT, why did you not sign up for the college prep classes?" I told him I had no interest in attending college. I explained that I tried out for middle school basketball but didn't make the team and had given up on my aspirations of playing college hoops for the UNC Tar Heels. He sat quietly for a moment, seemingly amused. Mr. Sellers spent the next few minutes explaining to me the benefits of attending college. He noted that I had good grades and an aptitude for math and science, and he encouraged me to consider becoming an engineer. Before I left his office, I had reenrolled in a straight run of college preparatory classes.

My guidance counselor's choice to authentically engage in a personalized way changed my life. He stirred my intellectual curiosity about science and math, which started a ripple effect. Four years later, this effect spread even further with my acceptance into NC State University as an engineering student. I graduated with a bachelor's degree in mechanical engineering and spent six years working as an engineer in the technology and communication industries. I eventually attended

UNC–Chapel Hill, not to play basketball but to receive a master's degree in business administration.

Mr. Sellers took just a few minutes to set that ripple effect into motion, yet it changed the trajectory of my life! It is also called the butterfly effect, and this means a lot to us at The Lincoln Center for Family and Youth. So much so that we made a plaque and hung it in the main corridor of our office space next to a large graphical display of the Lorenz attractor, as shown below.

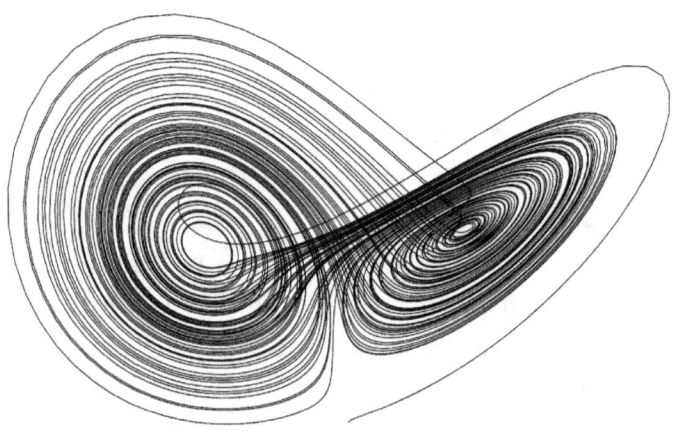

The accompanying text states:

> *This display is an artistic representation of TLC's vision statement, which is rooted in the butterfly effect.*
>
> *Founded in 1963 by mathematician and meteorologist Edward Lorenz, the Lorenz attractor is one of the most iconic images of*

> *Chaos theory, illustrating the phenomenon commonly known as the Butterfly Effect.*
>
> *The Butterfly Effect embodies a property of chaotic systems by which small variations in initial conditions can lead to large-scale changes in the future state of the system. The phenomenon is named partly after the three-dimensional representation of the mathematical equation and its resemblance to the wings of a butterfly. In addition, the example of the butterfly is used as a metaphor to illustrate how minor perturbations, such as a butterfly flapping its wings, can cause a tsunami on the other side of the world.*
>
> *At TLC, the butterfly effect reverberates throughout our entire organization as we aim to transform lives and communities—* one choice, one moment, one connection at a time. *Every relationship matters. Every choice counts. The smallest act or service provided can produce an enormous impact and literally change the world.*

Mr. Sellers was a transformational leader working in education. He embodied what we, at The Lincoln Center, call Transformational Education—a model of education in which teachers embrace the role of leader and strive to positively influence students both academically and socio-emotionally.

Transformational Education (TE) leans heavily on the concepts of Transformational Leadership (TL). TL offers solid building blocks for change through the influence of leaders; we apply these ideas to *the classroom*, exploring the relationship between teacher behaviors, school climate, student wellness, and performance outcomes.

TE is a unique model because it focuses on the tremendous power and influence of *the teacher* as the influential leader. This book will describe the compelling and robust effects of TE on student performance, realized when transformational teacher leadership is maximized in a supportive school climate.

"Leadership" is a buzzword that has topped the charts for decades now. Extensive research studies, programs, and educational sources have been dedicated to organizational leadership. What we know for sure is that leadership involves *influence*. There are many ideas about how this influence is carried out, which is also true in the field of education. As educators and parents, you have likely discussed instructional leadership,[1] or transformational school leadership,[2] based on the widely researched theory of TL. Core characteristics of TL include:

1. *Idealized influence*—increasing others' commitment to a compelling vision

2. *Inspirational motivation*—motivating followers to accomplish shared values and goals

3. *Individual consideration*—providing empathy and individual support

4. *Intellectual stimulation*—developing others' intellectual capacities for higher performance[3]

It is easy to see why TL might be applied to the school setting. These are potent capabilities in the hands of school leaders to foster an environment of inspiration, collaboration, and progress. In the field of education, TL has traditionally been regarded as a leadership approach employed by superintendents and principals. In this book, *teacher leadership matters most because, ultimately, it is the teacher who is in the best position to influence student outcomes.* This book proposes a new, teacher-centric leadership model that prescribes four values-based behaviors that educators can embody daily in their classrooms. These behaviors, when coupled with a supportive school climate, can have a significant impact on students' wellness and performance. We call this model Transformational Education.

The TE Model

Before we explore the model in detail, let's pause to consider our purpose and its significance. We'll begin with a simple exercise. Take a deep breath and clear your mind. Now, recall a teacher whose influence, whether subtle or profound, shifted your perspective, revealed a hidden aspect of yourself, or set your life on a new path. That teacher's impact is the reason we're here, and over the next four chapters, we'll examine the model that fosters such transformational change.

In discussing the TE model, it's essential to start with a fundamental, albeit frequently unspoken, truth about every school: *teachers are pivotal leaders within their schools and classrooms*. Therefore, we'll once again draw from TL theory, adapting the four tenets of TL[4] to better suit a classroom context.

Teachers influence students via four main paths, starting with *idealized influence*, which provides a compelling vision, sets high standards for emulation, serves as a role model for students, demonstrates high moral standards, and puts students' needs first. Second, *inspirational motivation* engages students in shared goals, provides meaning and challenge to their work, and inspires enthusiasm and optimism. Third, *individual consideration* provides empathy and support to students, addressing their needs and interests while coaching and mentoring them to develop new skills. Lastly, *intellectual stimulation* generates innovation and creativity as well as develops students' intellectual capacities for higher performance.[5]

It's worth pausing to acknowledge the substantial research supporting these ideals in school leadership. Studies show that when principals employ TL, it positively impacts student engagement and achievement—a welcome finding. Furthermore, significant evidence indicates improvements in student motivation, satisfaction, efficacy, and commitment.[6] The effectiveness of transformational school leadership is evident not only in principals but also in teachers who, as direct leaders of students, apply TL principles.

Leadership embodies the power to influence, and educators wield this authority within the classroom setting. Although further research is warranted, initial studies link the adoption of TL behaviors by teachers to enhanced student engagement and a positive classroom experience,[7] as well as an active student voice in deciding classroom activities.[8]

Mr. Sellers was neither a principal nor a teacher, yet he wielded great influence as the school's guidance counselor. Any school staff member, paid or volunteer, can have a significant impact on a student's life. Whether an administrator, teacher, counselor, coach, or cafeteria or custodial staff, anyone can make a significant difference in the life of a student—one moment, one choice, one connection at a time. Although this book is geared toward teachers in an educational context, the principles of TL are useful for anyone trying to make a difference in the lives of others, whether inside or outside the classroom.

The components of the TE model are *teacher behaviors, school climate, student wellness, and student performance*. Let's take a look at each.

1. **Teacher behaviors** include four teacher leadership practices: authentic engagement, meaning making, personalized support, and stimulating curiosity. These action-oriented values can have a significant impact on student outcomes, assuming they are reinforced by the school's climate. These teacher behaviors, which are rooted in TL theory and reimagined in a classroom setting, are shown in table 1 and explored in more detail in chapter 1 of this book.

Table 1: *Transformational Education Teacher Behaviors*

Transformational Leadership (TL)	Transformational Education (TE)	TE Teacher Behaviors
Idealized influence	Authentic engagement	Connect genuinely with students without judgment; model positive interactions in a protective environment
Inspirational motivation	Meaning making	Help students find meaning in their choices; appreciate their progress and become intentional in their identified purpose
Individual consideration	Personalized support	Adjust to students' strengths, needs, and goals so that they feel safe and are able to heal, grow, and learn
Intellectual stimulation	Stimulating curiosity	Challenge students to solve problems in new ways; foster introspection and engagement with themselves and others

2. **School climate** includes three important factors of organizational culture: classroom support, kindness, and aesthetic guidance. These cultural factors can affect the teacher's influence on student outcomes. Chapter 2 defines each of these concepts and provides examples of how both administrators and teachers can improve school climate.

3. **Student wellness** includes three primary student outcome measures: student connectedness, self-efficacy, and socio-emotional well-being. These student-centric outcomes are important antecedents for student performance and will be further explored in chapter 3.

4. **Student performance** includes three secondary outcome measures: student engagement, academic performance, and prosocial behaviors. These measures, discussed in chapter 4, are perhaps the three most commonly measured outcomes in schools (i.e., attendance, behavior, grades); however, they are significantly affected by teacher leadership behaviors, school climate, and student wellness.

Please examine figure 1 before proceeding, as I will discuss in more detail each of the four components of TE in the following chapters of this book. This depiction is adopted from a graphical representation of the TE model featured in a published concept paper, "A Proposed Model for Transformational Education," that describes the relationships among teacher behaviors, school climate, student wellness, and student performance.[9]

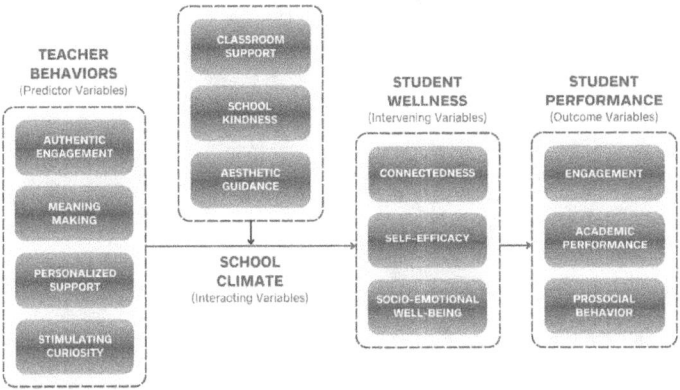

Figure 1: *Relationships among variables in the Transformational Education model*

As this book unfolds, you will see that these tried-and-true characteristics of TL serve as a *strong foundation* for TE. Throughout the book, I will include short testimonials from students, parents, and partners of The Lincoln Center, as well as my own personal stories of transformational educators like Mr. Sellers and others who significantly impacted my life. In sharing these personal stories, I hope to highlight how pivotal moments can profoundly shape one's life and career. These experiences have been crucial to my own development, and I am dedicated to fostering similar transformative moments for students everywhere. Finally, please note that while all the stories within these pages reflect true events and actual testimonials, certain names have been altered. Moreover, minor grammatical, content, and structural adjustments have been made to the testimonials to improve clarity, consistency, and readability.

Chapter 1

Teacher Behaviors: The Origin of the Ripple

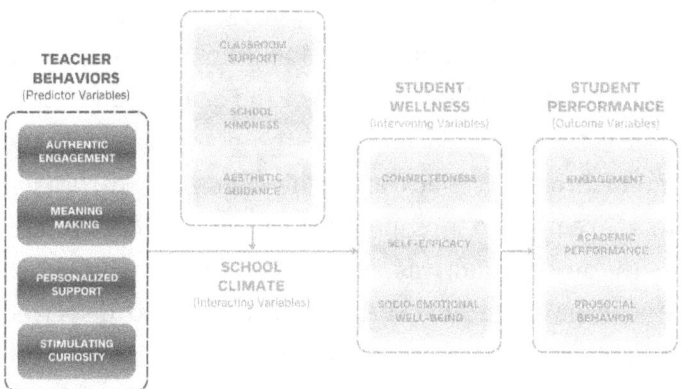

The world of Dungeons & Dragons was an escape for a doodling kid with some imagination and a mechanical pencil. I spent hours creating images of elves, halflings, and orcs from the D&D *Player's Handbook* and *Monster Manual*. I have great memories of sketching these fantasy characters in elementary and middle school. I believed I was talented; if true, it was due in part to my parents' artistic gifts. My mother was an oil painter who loved to work with natural landscapes and portraits. My father created award-winning, museum-like exhibits of animals in their natural habitats. It appeared the artistic gene was passed on to me.

Influenced by a mixture of nature and nurture, I loved drawing . . . until I landed in my ninth-grade English class. It was the spring semester of my freshman year. My classmates and I were working on a free verse lyric poetry assignment; I was entirely invested. For the project, I was writing about the paradoxical character of the natural world and how it can be both serene and tumultuous, ordered and chaotic, and beautiful yet terrible. To illustrate the poem, I sketched a monochromatic, black-and-white image of a tornado that exemplified this paradox. A path of destruction in the foreground was juxtaposed with an untouched landscape in the background. The tornado displayed randomness but also had a discernible structure. Both the poem and the drawing were designed to elicit mixed emotions. I put a lot of thought and effort into that artwork, vividly remembering the details decades later.

Toward the end of class, the teacher walked up and down the aisles, offering feedback on the students' poetry and artwork. He glanced at my drawing and said, "I don't like it; it's too dark and chaotic. I'd like you to redo it." He moved on.

Feeling disheartened, I returned home and sought my mother's help for the assignment, sharing that the teacher was looking for something more vibrant, cheerful, and optimistic. My mom then crafted a motivational and uplifting poem, extolling the virtues of hard work. To complement it, she illustrated a colorful robin, perched on a split rail fence, with a worm in its beak, and fittingly titled it "The Early Bird and the Worm." Admittedly, I admired the work for its paradoxical nature, appreciating the contrast between the uplifting message and the less fortunate implication for the worm.

Despite the worm's grim fate, the teacher approved. In fact, he liked it so much that he tacked it on the wall near the entrance of the classroom, alongside a few other "cheery" pieces. My mom's early-bird robin stared at me for months, persistently reminding me of my "failure" and the teacher's disapproval.

A ripple effect.

The moment my nature-tornado poem hit the trash can, I lost my enthusiasm for the arts. Just as a tornado quickly retreats into the atmosphere after wreaking havoc on the ground, my zeal for artistic expression also vanished. As time passed, my interest and involvement in the arts dwindled, and by the end of high school, I had ceased doodling and drawing entirely, never to resume.

Viewing this incident through the lens of adulthood, rather than the eyes of a sensitive and impressionable teenager, is crucial. My English teacher was not only a competent teacher but also a compassionate individual.

He would probably be surprised and disheartened to realize that this single incident has lingered in my memory for so many years. It's important to acknowledge our shared humanity, recognizing that our words and deeds can have unforeseen effects but also understanding and forgiving others and ourselves for our past missteps and regrets. Embracing these experiences as opportunities for growth allows us to move forward with wisdom and empathy.

For impressionable youth, teachers often set ripples in motion that advance for years, decades, and even generations. Teachers have the power to affect the lives of students positively, but sadly, negative swells are just as potent. Our goal at The Lincoln Center is to create long-lasting ripples of change in a positive direction. To do this, we must start with teacher behaviors.

Teachers' leadership determines many outcomes for schools and students. When teachers employ the practices we advocate in Transformational Education (TE), students feel more connected to each other and experience a greater sense of community. They have an overall increased sense of well-being and, in turn, learn more.[10] These are the type of results that every educator hopes for, and these are the ultimate goals of education. In short, the behaviors of teachers are crucial to achieving the outcomes that we strongly desire for every student. Rooted in Transformational Leadership (TL) theory and vital to the TE model, the four teacher behaviors are:

1. Authentic Engagement
2. Meaning Making
3. Personalized Support
4. Stimulating Curiosity

These four effectual behaviors align with the proven concepts of TL and those found to be impactful in project-based learning literature.[11] Notably, these behaviors also influence school climate and student behaviors.[12] TE integrates these insights to establish a comprehensive and holistic model that connects these valuable behavioral practices with progressively positive student outcomes.

1.1 Authentic Engagement

We learn best when we are intrinsically motivated, driven by our own desire to learn, interest in the subject, and enjoyment of the experience. Authentic engagement, the first of the four teacher behaviors in TE, seeks to foster meaningful motivation by minimizing extrinsic controls that rely on rewards and punishments. Instead, TE teachers aim to cultivate internal motivators, such as a love of learning or a genuine interest in a subject. This approach helps students value learning for its own merits, independent of external rewards like prizes, tokens, or even grades.

This vision is appealing to anyone devoted to education. But how do we achieve it? Let's adapt the business concept of "idealized influence" from TL for educational settings. Idealized influence occurs when teachers serve as role models, displaying commitment and enthusiasm for learning objectives. By exemplifying these qualities, teachers earn their students' admiration and trust. Believing deeply in the value of education and their teaching goals, these educators inspire similar feelings and behaviors in their students, both through direct instruction and by example. They demonstrate confidence in the learning process, express high regard for their learning community, and consistently act in the best interests of their students and the classroom.

My experience in ninth-grade English class was disheartening at that moment because I approached the poetry project with genuine interest and intrinsic motivation. My perception of a narrow, critical, and callous interaction with the teacher transformed my natural enthusiasm into feelings of disillusionment and caution. While I may have lost my zeal for artistic expression, those formative experiences have informed my work in TE. This encounter has shaped my conviction that fostering authentic engagement in the classroom not only enriches the learning environment but also serves as a foundational pillar for a more effective and comprehensive educational model.[13]

While verbal communication is essential in this role-modeling behavior, nonverbal cues are also impactful.

Teachers' reactions to student responses to lesson elements may matter even more than the content of those responses. Conveying genuine surprise and interest, sincere listening, and fostering meaningful dialogue create a more interactive environment and support learning.[14] It should be no surprise that authentically engaged instruction increases student engagement and achievement.[15] Furthermore, our lived experience with TE at The Lincoln Center suggests that authentic engagement positively influences students' wellness and fosters a sense of connectedness to the teacher and the school.

Throughout this book, I will share brief testimonials from students, parents, and partner organizations, providing insights into how TE has impacted their individual lives and the community.

Client Testimonials

I completed my senior year of high school at TLC, and I cannot express enough how wonderful my experiences were. Every teacher and staff member was so unbelievably friendly and approachable. Their program and focus points were great for the students. The amount of time and consideration put into acquiring these teachers did not go unnoticed. I became very close with each and every one, as they truly showed care for their students' lives as a whole, beyond the classroom. I made connections there that I still keep in contact with years after graduating.

—Graduate, TLC Leadership Academy

Compared to the other nontraditional facilities we toured, TLC was the ONLY place I considered sending my daughter. It's a clean, upbeat, and positive learning environment. The teachers are friendly and come up with creative ways to engage the students. They provide individual attention, catering to each student's educational needs. They also take the kids on many educational field trips, which my daughter really enjoyed.

—Parent, TLC Leadership Academy

1.2 Meaning Making

In my first year of high school, I was handpicked by my math teacher, Mr. Southern, to provide tutoring services to another student. He recognized that I had not only an aptitude for math but also, more importantly, an eagerness to learn. Mr. Southern knew that one of the best ways to learn something was to teach it. Furthermore, he understood that a passion for learning often translates into a passion for teaching, so he asked me to become a tutor. I agreed without even knowing which student I was to tutor; it turned out she was one of the most popular girls in school! She eventually became the cheerleading captain, homecoming queen, and prom queen. I tutored her for the next four years of high school. It was a mutually beneficial relationship; she improved her math skills (and grades), while my social standing improved.

But most importantly, tutoring strengthened my love for learning and cultivated a desire to become an educator. Mr. Southern helped me discover what is meaningful to me: a higher purpose, a calling. Though I couldn't put words to it at the time, I understood my life's mission: to transform lives and communities—one moment, one choice, one connection at a time.

Teachers stand as the true leaders within schools, possessing a more direct capacity than administrators to shape student experiences. When teachers, *as leaders*, adopt certain behaviors, they become transformational educators. Now that we understand authentic engagement, the first core teacher behavior for TE, let's move on to the second: **meaning making**.

Meaning making is grounded in inspiration and motivation. Inspiration activates new possibilities in our minds and allows us to rise above our ordinary experiences; inspiration also mobilizes students away from apathy and changes how they view their capabilities. Similarly, we think of motivation as the positive push that launches, guides, and sustains goal-oriented behaviors. It helps us get to the gym, try a new recipe, paint with watercolors, or finally submit that application we have been staring at for weeks. In short, motivation causes us to act in a way that gets us closer to our goals.

Since TE is a reworking of the building blocks of TL, *meaning making* is to the educator what *inspirational motivation* is to the business leader. Corporate leaders have a clear vision that they articulate to followers; then, they ignite the passion and motivation in followers to fulfill these goals for the company. When a teacher is a leader with clear learning goals for the classroom and can express this vision in a way that excites and engages the students, the group will experience higher performance levels.[16]

The meaning-making component of TE provides the educational inspiration that helps students to effectively interpret information and data, historical and current events, objects, language, or anything else in light of their previous knowledge and experience. Transformational meaning making occurs when a teacher leads and communicates excellence while taking the time to honestly focus on the value of the student and the learning goal at hand; inspirational teacher behavior goes hand in glove with authentic engagement to create motivation. Motivation also becomes a reality when teachers unite students to achieve essential and shared learning goals.

Meaning making is a critical process that involves guiding students to comprehend the significance of their decisions, along with the values and meanings these decisions embody. This concept is closely linked to the cultivation of prosocial values and the promotion of cooperation.[17] Prosocial values are those beliefs that cherish the concern and care for the well-being of others. These values translate to constructive behaviors or voluntary actions intended to improve another person's welfare. Prosocial behaviors include kindness, helping, caring, comforting, cooperating, and protecting. I didn't understand much about prosocial behavior when I was in ninth grade, but I'm certain Mr. Southern did. The enduring impact of his encouragement to assist a fellow student continues to ripple in my life, manifesting in an ongoing dedication to education and teaching.

Meaning making is a crucial component of leadership. As leaders, teachers guide students to explore prosocial values through action, including collaborative and helping behaviors. A key goal of teacher leadership is to continuously create meaning in students' lives—a behavior necessary for positive change at the classroom level.[18] It creates purpose by aligning individuals' goals, resulting in intrinsic motivation and commitment. I will reflect again on my free verse poem project, which negatively illustrates this point. In my ninth-grade classroom, the *lack of meaning-making teacher leadership* discouraged my artistic efforts and had a strong and effective result, but *in the opposite direction*. Instead of inspiring and motivating, the teacher's leadership practices extinguished my commitment to the learning goals. However, when positively structured, meaning-making behaviors of teachers can lead to beneficial outcomes and increased student engagement.

In the dyadic relationship between principals and teachers, the display of meaning-making behaviors of principals leads to increased teacher commitment.[19] The findings from principal-as-leader studies, while not surprising, hold exciting and promising implications for applying the same principle to teacher-student interactions. Although research on teachers as leaders is sparse, limited studies have shown that teachers who engage in meaning making significantly enhance students' sense of community.[20] Students guided by transformational, meaning-making teachers develop a heightened awareness of their prosocial actions and experience a strong sense of care and support for one another. Additionally, these students perceive themselves as essential contributors to the decision-making process within the classroom. The experience of collaboration and helping others, fostered by meaning-making teachers, equips students for successful futures in their families, colleges, workplaces, and communities. Our experience at The Lincoln Center, where schools have adopted TE, corroborates these insights.

Meet April

The fifth grade ushered in many changes for 10-year-old April. She walked up the steps in early September to the enormous middle school building. It was thrilling and terrifying, full of new students, teachers, smells, and lockers!

Everything might have been great if it wasn't for the new eyeglasses. At lunch on the third day, a group of girls called April "four-eyes." Next, it was "teacher's pet." It might have been a disaster if not for Ms. Biler.

Ms. Biler changed everything. Her class was safe; it was like a family. Ms. Biler learned their names in one day and seemed happy to see the students each morning. She loved books and got so excited when a new box of classroom books arrived that the students gathered around to see what was coming out of the crate. By the time a third box was delivered, the kids actually cheered. After lunch, Ms. Biler would read for 10 minutes, but she always snuck in an extra two minutes.

April had always been a straight-A student, so when she earned one C in the third marking period, Ms. Biler noticed; this encounter changed April's perspective on teachers and education forever.

Meet April (continued)

It happened during a parent-teacher conference. Instead of informing April's parents about her C grade, Ms. Biler asked April to share her own reflections with her parents and explain what led to the unhappy C and what April needed to do to improve in the fourth marking period. At that moment, April felt more responsible for her education than ever before. She began to understand the power of reflection, goals, and improvement. A meaning-making teacher challenged April to actively participate in her own academic process and be accountable for her outcomes for the first time. Even in the fifth grade, she began to see that education is not a spectator sport. It was impactful. She couldn't articulate this clearly for some years, but she caught it—a vision to reflect thoughtfully on her learning process. Ms. Biler was authentically engaged in April's journey; she motivated her students to take part in their learning with lasting impact.

Client Testimonials

TLC's Leadership Academy has been a godsend for my son. He needed more emotional support and a smaller class size than his public school could provide. He is now placed with fellow students who have similar struggles. For once, he feels like he is part of something. He is connected to them and can relate to his classmates. The group and individual counseling sessions the school provides have been wonderful.

—Parent, TLC Leadership Academy

When I first came to TLC, I was extremely nervous. However, after the first week in that environment, I knew I was surrounded by great teachers, counselors, and a principal who cared about the students—including me. This school made it easy to be more social because of the open layout and small class sizes. The teachers made going to class such an amazing experience, day after day. We had electives every Tuesday. This was great for me because it was like I had a mini break from all the schoolwork to explore classes like music, writing, and robotics. The group therapy sessions were very helpful because we did activities together where I received and gave help and feedback to the other students. We went on field trips once a month, and I can honestly say I explored more of what's out in the world

> in my one year at TLC than at any other time in my life. Being in this school has greatly contributed to this being the greatest year of my whole life so far.
> —Student, TLC Leadership Academy

> The Lincoln Center changes lives for the better. I could go on and on for days. My counselor and I still talk frequently three years after I graduated. Great organization! Thank you for all you've done for me and others. You are appreciated.
> —Graduate, TLC Leadership Academy

1.3 Personalized Support

Personalized support is the third behavior enacted by teacher-leaders in the TE model. Personalized support aligns with individual consideration, one of the four pillars of TL. When I think of personalized support, I think of Tony, my first executive leader and professional mentor. It was 1996, just a couple of years after I graduated from NC State. Our relationship launched my leadership journey at MCI Communications in Research Triangle Park, NC. Tony saw my potential and personally picked me to lead a special project to create the company's first intranet website. He also saw the desire to prove myself, a solid work ethic, and a strong interest in web technology. The successful launch of that intranet site began a ripple effect that significantly shaped my career path.

That first assignment led to another, which led to my first managerial position. Tony left MCI Communications and joined AT&T. He asked me to join him there, and I did. Moreover, he was instrumental in helping me achieve my MBA; he encouraged me, supported me, and paid for my degree while at AT&T. Decades later, I'm still in touch with Tony. I thank him often for the individual, personal support in those early, formative years of my career. Tony was indeed a transformational leader.

As an essential facet of effective leadership, individual consideration relies heavily on relationships; Tony's example demonstrates this so well. It occurs when transformational leaders genuinely regard followers' needs, concerns, and feelings. Individual attention to each follower is the fundamental element and key to drawing out their best efforts and maximizing their potential. This can become a reality through individual consideration because the leader is aware of the unique talents and abilities each follower brings to the workplace, team, or classroom. The leader is then positioned to support them in developing and demonstrating these skills and capabilities. Subsequently, followers experience intrinsic motivation and aspire to continue growing and developing. Examples of individual consideration in the workplace include one-on-one mentoring, delegating important decisions or tasks, or enjoying a higher level of communication with leaders. Individual consideration parallels personalized support in the TE model.

Personalized support involves promoting a warm and supportive classroom environment while actively encouraging student influence and participation. Teachers enacting this behavior provide for each student's needs and tailor instruction to their interests, fostering student growth and decision-making.[21] TE teachers attempt to meet each child's individual needs and stimulate each one to achieve learning goals and rise to life's challenges. Teacher-leaders who practice personalized support understand the value of prioritizing their time in a way that allows them to develop a personal connection with each student, regardless of their background, performance, or ability level.

Empathy is a vital ingredient of personalized support. A teacher-leader acting as a mentor or guide by attending to each follower's needs shows empathy for their students. Teachers skilled in demonstrating empathy and care become attuned to their students' feelings, recognizing that their individual needs differ. Empathetic teachers are active listeners; the transformational teacher listens to the concerns of each student-follower and provides support by being considerate of each person's situation and background. Empathy allows TE teachers to challenge students according to their talents and knowledge while recognizing their individual contributions to the group or class. This level of empathetic communication empowers students to make decisions and feel supported as they are implemented, aiding in student self-development and intrinsic motivation.

When I reflect back on my tutoring experience in high school math, I am reminded of the personalized support provided by Mr. Southern. His intervention was not merely academic; it was deeply personal. Recognizing my natural inclination toward mathematics and the potential for helping others to learn the subject, Mr. Southern created an opportunity that went beyond the confines of a traditional classroom. He saw a unique potential in me—not just as a student who could solve algebraic equations but as an individual who could inspire and elevate others. This tailor-made path he charted for me to become a tutor was his way of nurturing my teaching ability, acknowledging that the essence of education lies in its power to transform through personal connection. Moreover, his insight into how this role could enhance my social standing within the school community was a testament to his holistic concern for my development. Mr. Southern's intentional act of pairing me with a peer from a vastly different social circle was not incidental; it was a strategic move to enrich my high school experience in every facet. By doing so, he demonstrated the profound impact of personalized support in fostering not only academic growth but also personal well-being and social harmony. Through his actions, Mr. Southern affirmed that education at its best is a deeply individualized journey, where recognizing and cultivating personal gifts can lead to the most meaningful outcomes.

Personalized support naturally flows with the previous behaviors we have discussed, authentic engagement and meaning making, and I believe the positive effects on students are compounded. My personal experience with Mr. Southern affirms this assertion, as his personal support of my natural ability was a springboard into my professional life; research supports this as well. For example, one study revealed that personalized support resulted from authentically engaged classroom instruction, which in turn leads to higher levels of student engagement and achievement.[22] In addition, a second and recent study found that customized teacher support promoted engagement.[23] Still, other research has linked this support with reduced internalizing and school problems, as well as increased personal adjustment.[24] These studies suggest what we are also experiencing at The Lincoln Center: these behaviors link together naturally to create transformational classrooms.

When enacting personalized support, teacher-leaders become transformational educators who truly *transform* students and classrooms by focusing on students as individuals, motivating them to higher levels of performance, and, in the process, helping them develop their leadership potential. *Sincere* attention to individual students' emotional states, needs, and concerns will place teachers on a trajectory of high impact as leaders. When teachers intentionally prioritize relationships by demonstrating interest in each student's uniqueness and value, students have positive experiences of teacher-leaders. Students will forever carry memories of teachers who made a deliberate effort to know them as an individual and encouraged them to succeed.

Client Testimonials

TLC helped me to achieve my goal of graduating high school and prepared me for my life outside of school. I use the skills that the counseling staff has taught me in my everyday life, even now. They inspire the students to achieve their dreams and cater to every individual's specific educational needs.

—Student, TLC Leadership Academy

TLC has helped me with my struggles at school for about a year now. I am currently a senior with goals of graduating and going to college. The school has helped me, especially with how much support I get and how helpful the teachers are. Each individual here has their own needs; the school goes above and beyond to try and help everyone to the best of their ability. The counselors are always open to listening and working out any problems and are great listeners. All the staff members bring something different to the school, making it unique and a nice place to be.

—Student, TLC Leadership Academy

After visiting every alternative school in the area, nothing compared to TLC! They offer individual counseling once a week for each student. In addition, they have a group counseling session every day. They also have their off-site psychiatrist evaluate your child upon admission to the school and every year after that. They have the cutest therapy dogs that roam the schools daily, loving on all the students! They work closely with your child's outside therapists, counselors, psychiatrists, home school district, and, most importantly, parents! The teachers there are amazing and are all trained in trauma-informed care. The counselors there are involved in all the school-day activities; they are always available to talk to the students! And the staff have fantastic communication with the parents whenever it is needed.

—Parent, TLC Leadership Academy

Meet Andrea

Andrea desperately wanted to be a field hockey player in high school. A freshman at a prestigious Catholic girls' school, she watched the team stooping, passing, and celebrating on the turf; it looked really fun. She began to practice field hockey in her yard, and after months of shooting on her backyard goal and passing off the brick garage, she tried out for the team as a sophomore. This was risky; most girls started as freshmen and had played in middle school. Nevertheless, Andrea plucked up her courage and walked on. Tryouts were intense! She arrived home every day muddy, grass-stained, bruised, and exhausted. So it was no consolation that she made it to the final round before being cut; it was a hard blow.

Andrea let the emotional dust settle before trashing her stick and sadly joining the girls' track team as she'd done throughout middle school.

The cool thing in track and field was to be a sprinter. Everybody wanted to run the 100-meter dash in middle school. Andrea didn't have the speed for the short distance, but she ran it anyway. After one meet, Coach Jack pulled her aside and said, "Andrea, what about the 400- or 800-meter race? Maybe those distances would be a better fit for you." She stormed out, offended. Driving home, she had to

Meet Andrea (continued)

admit that it was frustrating and embarrassing to come in last in every 100 and 200.

Coach Jack began watching YouTube videos of great runners he thought had similar abilities as Andrea. He sent the helpful ones to her. Then Coach gave her his copies of How She Did It *and* Zola: The Autobiography of Zola Budd. *They were captivating.*

Without telling Coach, she went on several long-distance runs over the next month out of curiosity. Within weeks, she was hooked and told Coach, who smiled and signed her up for the 400 and the 800 at the next meet. She placed decently. With growing curiosity, together they signed her up to run the novice mile at championships. Andrea was just a sophomore and not officially on varsity, so this was a test for up-and-coming talent.

The workouts Coach Jack designed for her were intimidating. She worked hard; Coach was her biggest fan. Finally, all the jittery girls lined up in their school colors on race day. The gun cracked, and she was off with Coach's cheers chasing her down the lane. To their surprise, she placed second overall in the novice mile. Coach Jack went nuts! It was a defining moment in her life.

Meet Andrea (continued)

Junior year, Andrea decided to run cross-country in the fall and fell in love with distance running. She had a great career as an upperclassman and became the captain of her team during her senior year. After that, she went on to run cross-country in college. From cross-country, it was only a short step into cross-training and her ultimate love: the triathlon.

Andrea stayed connected to Coach Jack and her mentors, and after graduation, she became as an assistant coach at her high school. Andrea loved helping kids develop their running skills, providing new runners with the same guidance and support she'd received. She knew it would lead to personal growth and leadership development beyond running; that was so satisfying!

Coach Jack's interest, support, and encouragement were unforgettable. Running longer distances and embracing the sport of cross-country led Andrea to gain more meaning in her life than she ever could've imagined. She became an Ironman three times and a runner/triathlete at all distances. Yet Andrea still values her coaching years as some of the most special in her life. The butterfly effect led her into the wonderful world of coaching others!

1.4 Stimulating Curiosity

Stimulating curiosity is the fourth and final teacher behavior in the TE model. As the name suggests, the intention of stimulating curiosity is to elicit student thinking and idea expression.[25] Teachers who stimulate curiosity lead students toward two goals. First, they encourage students to think about *how and why*. Second, they instigate and build *curiosity* to clarify and solve problems. When I reflect on the value of intellectual stimulation, I'm reminded of two friends, Craig and Todd.

Although I was born and raised in the Bible Belt, my parents were agnostics; consequently, I had no exposure to any religious traditions growing up. After graduating from college and starting my professional career at IBM, a former college roommate, Craig, invited me to church. I told him I wasn't interested. He persisted for the next few weeks; one Sunday morning, he showed up unannounced at the Players Club (not kidding, that was the name of my apartment complex). I reluctantly attended. I was surprised to see that it was a large and thriving church with many young adults my age. I thought it was a good place to meet friends.

One of these new friends was Todd, who I later learned was one of the coleaders in the youth ministry. He approached me and started an authentic discussion; we talked about lots of topics that were important to me. He asked great questions, including questions of faith.

In a very gentle and nonjudgmental manner, he stirred my intellectual curiosity to learn more about *his faith*. That interaction sparked a multiyear journey to learn— not only about the Christian faith but also about all the other major religions of the world. I stuck around and eventually met my wife at that church a couple of years later, and we were married there. It makes me think about Craig's decision to pursue our friendship and continually invite me into something that was meaningful to him. I also remember Todd's decision to engage me in an intellectually stimulating discussion, which started a ripple effect that drastically and positively altered the trajectory of my life.

Stimulating curiosity is a slight shift from TL's conception of intellectual stimulation, in which the workplace leader employs this behavior to challenge followers to attain higher performance levels through innovation and creativity. Intellectual stimulation encourages followers to rethink and reinvent work habits and paths while looking for better ways to execute tasks. Challenging assumptions are approved by leaders who enact intellectual stimulation; they nurture and affirm independent thinking among followers. In this work culture, new ideas are welcome and met without criticism; unexpected events, problems, delays, and challenges are viewed by leaders and followers as learning opportunities.

In TE, stimulating curiosity corresponds to intellectual stimulation. Teachers function as transformational leaders by encouraging students to challenge assumptions, take risks, and collaborate. They recognize students' efforts toward stimulation, creativity, and innovation. Reflecting on my own experiences with dismissed artistic and poetic attempts, I am grateful that my youngest daughter, an aspiring illustrator, did not face similar rejection. Considering how deeply she took to heart the feedback from her teachers, and understanding the profound impact that stifling exploration and curiosity had on my own trajectory, I am overjoyed that her educators chose to nurture her artistic curiosity instead. They encouraged her to dive deeply into her creative talents, a practice we at The Lincoln Center passionately emulate with all of our students today.

At The Lincoln Center, we train teacher-leaders in ways that support and collaborate with their student-followers, encouraging them to explore new approaches to their music, storytelling, dance, scientific experiments, and everything else. They lead students to develop innovative ways of dealing with organizational issues in their peer group or team. Classrooms led by teachers who seek to stimulate curiosity are emboldened to think things out on their own. Independent thinking is supported so that students become autonomous and able to process the challenges in their lives.

This behavior has garnered attention from social scientists, and stimulating curiosity has been highlighted in education research.[26] One researcher examined how curiosity drives innovation and learning, emphasizing exploration rather than the accumulation of facts.[27] When stimulating curiosity has been enacted at the school leadership level, where the principal is the leader, it's been observed that an increased commitment results among teachers.[28] The same concrete student outcomes will occur in the classroom where the teacher is the leader.[29] Last, an exciting study that examined teacher leadership found that intellectual stimulation resulted in deep and strategic approaches to learning, resulting in student empowerment, which led to increased affective and cognitive growth.[30]

Transformational educators focus on student-followers, motivating them to high levels of performance and, in the process, help followers develop their leadership potential through the implementation of four impactful behaviors: authentic engagement, meaning making, personalized support, and stimulating curiosity. As a result, teacher-leaders will transform students' experience today, with positive effects rippling far into the future.

Chapter 2

School Climate: The Optimal Environment

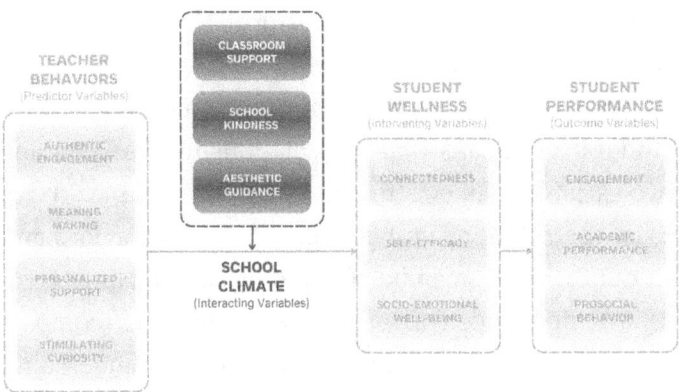

The teacher behaviors we have discussed take place *somewhere* in a real context.

That *somewhere* is a school context, of course. Yet never before has "school context" meant so many different things. For example, many families have a plethora of school options to choose from, spanning from traditional public schools, expensive college preparatory schools, public charter schools, online charter schools, faith-based schools, and homeschooling to alternative schools like the one we host at The Lincoln Center. Each of these educational contexts has a *school climate.*

The characteristic climate of a school is bound up with the individuals who constitute that school, and the behaviors of those individuals, teachers, administration, and staff have a tremendous influence on the school climate.

School climate connects teacher behaviors to student outcomes. In the Transformational Education (TE) model, school climate *moderates* the relationships between teacher behaviors and student wellness. Moderation means that the relationship between any two variables can be affected by a third variable. In this case, the relationship between teacher behaviors and student wellness can be affected by school climate.

We don't need to delve too deeply into complex research terminology, but it's essential to understand that in the TE model, school climate acts as a moderating variable, also known as an interacting variable. In other words, school climate *interacts with* teacher behaviors to affect student wellness. Specifically, interacting variables affect the strength and direction of the relationship between other variables, in this case, teacher behaviors and student outcomes. The downward arrow in the diagram at the start of this chapter reveals that school climate *acts upon or influences* the relationship between teacher behaviors and student outcomes—changing its strength and perhaps even the direction of the relationship. Researchers studying school climate have also revealed this connection, linking the environment to academic learning,[31] the socio-emotional well-being of students, and school connectedness.[32] School climate has been shown to *positively affect* students' engagement and achievement.

In the TE model, classroom support and school kindness are two factors contributing to school climate. They measure the socio-emotional or relational elements of the climate. A third factor, aesthetic guidance, describes how the physical school and classroom spaces shape the teaching and learning process. Aesthetic guidance also influences the students' sense of safety, the institutional environment, and the capacity to improve.

I hope you will take special note of the student testimonies I have included in this section. They are very persuasive because these factors significantly influence the student experience. Together, these mirror five themes that recur in studies surrounding school climate: safety, relationships, teaching and learning, institutional environment, and school improvement. In summary, school climate consists of **aesthetic guidance**, **school kindness**, **and classroom support**; the following three sections will address these three individually.

2.1 Classroom Support

Classroom support stands as a pivotal pillar within the triad that constitutes school climate. It refers to the empathetic and caring behaviors exhibited by the school toward the classroom environment; this empathy and care can flow toward students from teachers, staff, and other students. Empathy is the ability to *understand and share* the feelings of another; care is easy to understand and comes in many forms.

In caring school communities, when classroom support is effectively implemented, research has demonstrated a positive correlation with enhanced student academic achievements and socio-emotional health.[33] Supporting this, another study found that supportive classroom behaviors are part of a more extensive network of factors that contribute to student success, including self-efficacy.[34] Reflecting on chapter 1, it was noted that the teacher's role in facilitating *meaning making* notably strengthened students' sense of community. This aspect of classroom support amplified peer-to-peer encouragement, fostering an environment where students felt valued and supported by one another. Furthermore, it empowered students with a meaningful role in classroom decision-making processes. These experiences not only enrich the educational journey but also are invaluable in preparing students for success in various career paths, echoing the skills and attitudes prized in the professional world.

The influence of a peer support system on student experiences is profound. Recent observations have highlighted its crucial role within the classroom support framework, directly linking it to aspects of student wellness like feelings of connectedness and socio-emotional health.[35] As educators dedicated to nurturing the whole individual, it's imperative to heed research pointing toward enhancements in such broad areas as student wellness, integrating these insights into school practices wherever feasible.

Summarizing, classroom support is a key component in shaping a school's climate. The Transformational Education (TE) model underscores its significance by categorizing it as one of three dimensions of an interacting variable, school climate, that moderates the relationship between teacher actions and student wellness. There's a growing enthusiasm among educators to devise strategies that foster supportive learning environments. This endeavor is particularly emphasized at The Lincoln Center, where the impact is evident in student and parent testimonials.

Client Testimonials

Finding TLC for my son has been a godsend. He needed more emotional support and a smaller class size than his public school could provide. He is now with other students with similar struggles to which he can relate. He feels like a part of something for once. No other alternative school even came close to the amount of group and individual support they provide for their students.

—Parent, TLC Leadership Academy

TLC helped me so much, and it was a fantastic program. The therapists were outstanding, and I definitely was able to get the one-on-one attention that I needed. I never thought I would graduate high school. However, with the support I received in all of my TLC classes, I not only graduated but have gotten my life onto the right track and am even attending college! I love this organization. The staff is a bunch of great people as well!

—Graduate, TLC Leadership Academy

TLC is a much safer environment where I don't feel any harm will come my way. If I have any issues, there will always be someone to talk to and support me. Something unique about the school is the homework policy; being able to go home and not bring school stress home is very supportive, and I can complete all the curriculum. TLC is a school with better and more understanding staff, a supportive education plan, a nice setup, and the ability to talk to anyone at any time to help resolve issues.

> TLC provides a system that is safer, less stressful, and a more supportive learning experience than the average school can achieve.
> —STUDENT, TLC LEADERSHIP ACADEMY

Music and Mentoring

At TLC, learning occurs in many ways. One of the critical elements of student support in our programs is the relationships formed and nurtured through mentoring. We are intentional with our hiring and program planning to ensure that students can connect with and be guided by caring adults. This is more than just an added unexpected outcome of our school culture. It is a vital piece of the fabric of our design and is directly aligned with our vision to transform lives and communities—one moment, one choice, one connection at a time. Mentoring, formally and informally, occurs daily in all TLC programs. What is unique is that the joys of both the students and the staff are developed through mentoring.

Through the mentoring relationships with our Coatesville students, one of our team members discovered a mutual love of music with his students.

Music and Mentoring (continued)

Out of that connection, an innovative approach to mentoring was born. Our staff member approached the administration to ask whether he could pilot a new program that would allow music to be the catalyst for deepening the mentoring relationship with his students. This innovative idea was welcomed and celebrated by school leaders. The team member held his first "Music and Mentoring" session, utilizing some of his musical equipment from home. What resulted was an environment of trust because the adult had listened to the students. A mutually rewarding experience was developed because students and facilitators bonded over their love for the art of music. Relationships are powerful, mentoring is impactful, and the outcomes are certainly enhanced with the added soundtrack of music.

—TLC Staff Member

2.2 School Kindness

The term "kindness" is often reserved for individuals, soliciting encouragements from others to engage in *random acts of kindness* and prompting statements such as "Mrs. Jackson was kind to me." Associating kindness with an institution is not as common. However, this section will explore the notion of "school kindness."

In the context of TE, school kindness refers to the deliberate, altruistic actions aimed at benefiting others. These actions are viewed collectively and are characteristic of the entire school culture, not just a few individuals. Furthermore, these voluntary actions are not motivated by external factors such as rewards or punishments.[36]

When examining students' emotional state within their social contexts, evidence suggests that school kindness significantly enhances socio-emotional health and well-being.[37] Thus, when schools make a conscious decision to prioritize other-centered acts of kindness, it leads to a culture of kindness that, in turn, affects schools' overall social wellness. This notion is closely tied to the concept of classroom support, a crucial element within the trio of components that define the TE school climate framework.

Researchers have also observed the beneficial impact of school kindness on students' overall life satisfaction[38] and enhanced academic self-efficacy, which encompasses students' confidence in their intellectual abilities and their capacity to complete tasks effectively throughout their education.[39] Student self-efficacy also encapsulates confidence in their motivation, behaviors, and social skills essential for success in educational contexts. Interestingly, the positive influence of school kindness and climate extends beyond the educational setting, enriching students' overall life experiences.

School kindness fosters an environment where students are more likely to engage in prosocial behaviors, which are crucial for nurturing healthy interpersonal relationships. Prosocial behaviors include acts of cooperation, helping, comforting, sharing, and giving, among others. Creating a culture of kindness among students, staff, and community members acts as a catalyst for a socially and emotionally healthy environment that improves school outcomes.[40] More specifically, research has shown clear linkages between school kindness and students' cognitive, behavioral, and emotional engagement.[41] By adopting practices that foster a culture of kindness, schools provide a safe and nurturing environment that allows students to fully immerse themselves in their education. Considering the findings on classroom support, school kindness is positioned as the second dimension of school climate, the interacting variable that moderates the relationship between teacher actions and student wellness. Creating a culture of kindness is important to The Lincoln Center, as evidenced in the following student and parent testimonials.

Client Testimonials

TLC has been a tremendous help to my family! My son had difficulty early in his senior year of high school. He faced severe consequences at his area school, which could have led to expulsion. We were given a choice to stay at his area school or transfer to TLC to finish the year. We came for a visit, and I knew instantly that this was the place for him. The facility was state-of-the-art and had bright colors and cozy workspaces. The staff took an active interest in our visit and were very friendly. Once my son started attending school, he was immediately supported and encouraged by the wonderful staff. They went above and beyond to provide transportation to and from school, help him get his schoolwork caught up, accompany him to doctors' visits, assist him with college applications, and offer overall emotional and educational support. My son just graduated in June and was accepted to Rosemont College to pursue a four-year degree in accounting. TLC even awarded him with a four-year scholarship toward his college tuition! I do not doubt that the kind, fine folks at TLC were the deciding factor in helping him feel supported, stay focused, and set goals for his future. I will always be grateful for the staff at TLC, their commitment and kindness to the students, and their comprehensive program.

—Parent, TLC Leadership Academy

My nonprofit company currently works with The Lincoln Center to provide creative arts opportunities to their students. I am always impressed by how their team goes above and beyond to show kindness to others. They have grown in size and helped countless families in the community. I highly recommend them!

—TLC PARTNER ORGANIZATION

The Lincoln Center does exceptional work! As someone who has been working with youth for 15-plus years, I've never seen an organization provide such impactful programming and support for all types of youth. Unfortunately, far too often, youth with challenging backgrounds are forgotten. The assumption is made that they're bad kids. As adults, we forget how difficult life can be without the proper support and kindness to help us navigate life. We forget that with consistent love and support, youth can truly accomplish what they set their minds to. The Lincoln Center consistently offers love, kindness, and support to ensure that no child is left behind—allowing all youth to fulfill their purpose. I consider any kid lucky if they can work with the wonderful, caring staff at The Lincoln Center.

—TLC PARTNER ORGANIZATION

2.3 Aesthetic Guidance

The concept of school climate encompasses the entire essence of the school community, representing the collective perception of the school's atmosphere. A crucial component of this climate is the physical presentation of the school space, which forms the third pillar of what defines school climate. Within the TE framework, this aspect is identified as "aesthetic guidance." This concept demands significant attention for its impactful role in shaping the learning environment and influencing student experiences.

The term "aesthetic" might present challenges in pronunciation and spelling, yet it encapsulates precisely the concept we at The Lincoln Center aim to convey. This multifaceted word carries several interrelated meanings. Initially, it pertains to a philosophical branch concerned with the essence of beauty and art, emphasizing discernment and enjoyment of beauty. Additionally, aesthetic describes a specific inclination toward or methodology in appreciating what appeals to the five senses. Broadly, it signifies what is conventionally considered beautiful or appealing to sensory perception.

In the context of education, *aesthetic guidance* refers to the efforts made to create appealing sensory experiences that foster student learning in the classroom. Academic researchers have defined aesthetics as the "felt meaning generated from sensory perceptions, involving subjective, tacit knowledge rooted in feeling and emotion."[42] Sensory perception flows inward through touch, sight, hearing, smell, and taste. Perceptions travel to the brain through the nervous system to create felt meaning. This meaning or communication involves learning through understood or implied means without facts, data, and knowledge being stated; it includes subjective learning influenced by personal feelings, tastes, or opinions. While capturing the essence of aesthetics in words can be challenging, its application has proven to be a profoundly effective approach at The Lincoln Center, underscoring its value despite the complexities involved in fully grasping and utilizing it.

Educational environments, shaped by aesthetic considerations, exert both a direct and indirect influence on students, with research indicating significant positive outcomes. These include enhanced abilities in critical thinking and creative problem-solving.[43] Studies have shown that positive aesthetic experiences are strong predictors of student learning and achievement. Notably, specific physical aspects of the classroom environment, such as lighting and seating configurations, play crucial roles in influencing students' learning behaviors and academic success.[44] To further elaborate on this topic, it's worth considering the perspective of educator David Fenner, who proposed a four-dimensional comprehensive framework for understanding the impact of aesthetics in educational settings.

1. **Object directness**, where the object, for example, the classroom or school space, directs the individual's attention in ways that help the individual sense that things will resolve positively.

2. **Felt freedom**, in which the object or space enables the individual to sense the ability to make choices freely.

3. **Detached affect**, whereby the object or space enables the individual to gain emotional distance from things that frighten or oppress them.

4. **Active discovery**, where the object or space challenges the individual to discover new connections and solve problems creatively.

At The Lincoln Center (TLC), we've adopted this theoretical framework to deeply explore how students interact with and respond to aesthetic elements. Both our research and anecdotal observations confirm that aesthetic experiences significantly boost student wellness and performance. Our TLC schools are designed with an open layout that eliminates traditional walls, fostering a fluid and spacious learning environment. Rather than standard desks, students can choose from bean bags, floor cushions, or standing desks, which enhances comfort and flexibility in their learning postures. We've also created designated spaces stocked with art supplies, books, and comfortable seating, promoting quiet reflection and creativity. Additionally, we use color psychology extensively in our facilities; energizing colors like yellow and orange are used to foster creativity, while calming hues of blue and green help maintain a peaceful learning atmosphere conducive to well-being.

In summary, the TE model presents a cohesive narrative of how transformational teacher leadership directly benefits students. Grounded in rigorous research and proven leadership principles, this educational paradigm positions teachers at the forefront of leadership. The model becomes particularly compelling when teachers apply the discussed behaviors within an environment characterized by support, kindness, and aesthetic guidance, fostering an environment that nurtures student wellness and improves academic outcomes.

Client Testimonials

Our company partnered with The Lincoln Center to implement a real estate project to expand TLC's physical presence in the community. TLC's commitment to providing student-centered learning space was evident throughout the entire project. Their new school is unlike any other. Its large, open, colorful, nontraditional design inspires students to create and collaborate in a safe environment. TLC's new learning space is truly impressive. Working with TLC's administrative team was a pleasure, and we hope to collaborate with them again on future projects.

—TLC PARTNER ORGANIZATION

Our company has worked with The Lincoln Center over the past year and a half, as they've upgraded their space and surroundings to better serve the community they represent. In addition, their professional and well-rounded staff shows how deeply they care about today's youth by providing the best possible environment for education and mentoring.

—TLC PARTNER ORGANIZATION

This organization is so professional and well run. Every single person is professional, kind, and helpful. As I have worked closely with them in improving their interior spaces, I have witnessed the depth of commitment and innovation for the community and the families and youth they serve. I recommend that anyone needing a nontraditional learning facility contact The Lincoln Center. I know you will be impressed. Every child deserves the best chance to excel. TLC will provide the opportunity.

—TLC PARTNER ORGANIZATION

> TLC stands out positively against my last school for many reasons. First, TLC has a calmer, open setting where stress is minimal. It is the opposite of an anxiety-inducing environment (that feels more like a jail than anything else). Second, it contrasts the bland rooms and white concrete I am used to. Third, TLC has an open and more colorful environment that is more pleasing and welcoming.
>
> —STUDENT, TLC LEADERSHIP ACADEMY

CHAPTER 3

Student Wellness: The First Ripples

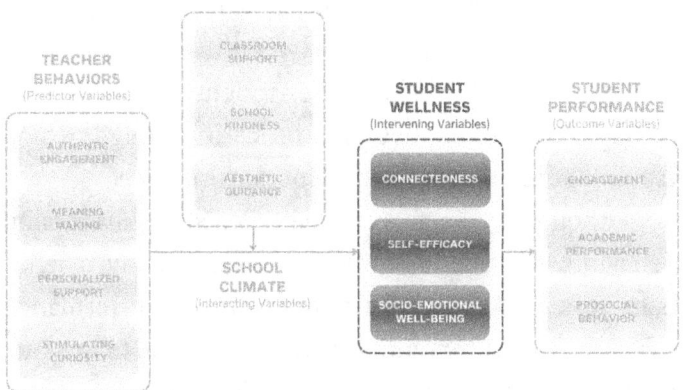

We began this conversation about Transformational Education (TE) by declaring that teachers are leaders and examining the teacher behaviors that positively transform the students' educational experience. These behaviors are the predictor or independent variables that set TE into motion. Teacher behaviors predict higher levels of student wellness outcomes, which in turn predict higher levels of student performance.

In this section, I will unpack the three factors that make up the **student wellness** intervening variable. Also known in scholarly research as mediating variables, intervening variables *account for the relationship (show the connection)* between the predictor variable and the outcome variable. In this model, TE behaviors of teachers *account for* increased student wellness, which in turn *accounts for* the student performance outcomes that all educators desire. In other words, student wellness *shows the connection* between teacher behaviors and student performance. The student wellness intervening variable defines the process through which teacher behaviors affect student performance.

Although transformational teacher leadership behaviors impact student performance directly, teacher behaviors also indirectly affect student performance through the intervening variable. Specifically, student wellness partially accounts for the relationship between teacher actions in the classroom and academic performance. In the TE model, the three factors or components of student wellness are connectedness, self-efficacy, and socio-emotional well-being.

3.1 Connectedness

Connectedness is the first of the three components of student wellness. This construct refers to the extent to which students feel part of the community within their school, family, and friends. Connectedness comprises students' internal experiences, perceptions, and feelings about school. These encompass important notions that include a sense of belonging, relationships with staff and other students, and the feeling that learning is a priority.

Significant correlations have been identified between certain teacher behaviors and enhanced student connectedness within the school community. A sense of belonging is linked to numerous positive outcomes, including prosocial behavior, motivation to learn, and other student outcomes. Studies show that connectedness leads to improved student engagement, active participation in classroom activities, and overall academic success. For example, one study emphasized the important role of adult mentorship in significantly boosting students' feelings of belonging with their family, peers, and overall school community.[45] Another study revealed a reduction in depression levels among individuals with higher levels of connectedness. Adult mentoring provided by teachers, guidance counselors, school principals, coaches, and other staff members has been shown to offer significant benefits, including feelings of enhanced personalized academic and socio-emotional support.[46]

In the educational journey, a student's feeling of connectedness to their school community is not just beneficial; it's transformative, especially during critical transitions such as moving from primary to secondary education.[47] This deep sense of belonging profoundly impacts socio-emotional well-being, laying a foundation for personal development and academic achievement. In this context, connectedness not only enriches the educational experience but also acts as a catalyst for well-being, setting the stage for effective teaching strategies to directly enhance student performance. At The Lincoln Center, a deliberate emphasis on bolstering student connectedness highlights its critical role in promoting success across all grade levels. Within the TE model, connectedness is identified as a key element of student wellness. This intervening variable facilitates the positive impact of transformational teaching on student outcomes, illustrating its indispensable role in the educational ecosystem.

The Choice to Connect

In a remarkable turn of events one November day, the presence of two local police officers on our campus, there to assist with a nonemergency situation, set the stage for an unforgettable moment of connection. As these officers were leaving, an unexpected invitation from one of our students to join a basketball game transformed an ordinary day into something extraordinary. Initially hesitant, the student was taken aback when one of the officers

The Choice to Connect (continued)

enthusiastically accepted the challenge, sparking a ripple of excitement.

What unfolded next was nothing short of magical: a game of basketball that brought together students and officers, with laughter, camaraderie, and an incredible dunk that captivated onlookers. This friendly match went beyond the game; it was a triumph of human connection over preconceived notions. In this singular moment, a student extended an olive branch of trust, an officer embraced it wholeheartedly, and both discovered the immense value of taking time to connect.

The powerful message from this day resonates far beyond the basketball court: it's the small acts of kindness and the willingness to engage that can bridge worlds, alter perceptions, and echo throughout the community, reminding us all of the profound impact of our choices and actions.

—TLC Staff Member

Client Testimonials

My experience at TLC's Leadership Academy has been great! I've connected with students, teachers, and staff because everyone is friendly and helpful. In my opinion, I am really feeling well, tied in, and excelling here. This is a great school, and I would recommend it to other students who need the support of caring staff and counselors or feel lost in their current school. I look forward to spending another great year with the staff and students next year!

—STUDENT, TLC LEADERSHIP ACADEMY

I like being a student at this school because the teachers connect with us; they address our specific needs and personalize our instruction based on how we learn. In addition, the staff members are all very nice and supportive. TLC has helped me mature and develop as a young adult and complete my academic coursework. I usually am not one to feel close to the people at school, but TLC has changed my perception of school drastically. I am now earning better grades, have improved my attendance, and will graduate on time.

—STUDENT, TLC LEADERSHIP ACADEMY

3.2 Self-Efficacy

Self-efficacy, the second of the three components of student wellness, is crucial in fostering educational success. Broadly, self-efficacy is a person's belief in their ability to achieve a goal or complete a task. In an educational context, it refers to a student's belief in their own ability to successfully execute tasks and reach goals specifically related to their learning and academic performance. This concept is integral to how students perceive their capacity to handle classroom assignments, manage their study time effectively, participate in discussions, and cope with academic challenges. Self-efficacy influences not only their motivation to engage in learning activities but also their resilience in the face of setbacks and their overall academic achievement. Students with high self-efficacy are more likely to set ambitious goals, persist through difficulties, and achieve higher academic standards because they believe in their ability to succeed.

Self-efficacy is closely linked to cognitive engagement, highlighting that students' belief in their ability to succeed is a crucial factor in how actively they engage with their learning tasks. Research indicates that self-efficacy is a more reliable predictor of academic performance than students' past achievements.[48] This suggests that a student's confidence in their capabilities can enhance their focus, effort, and persistence in educational activities, leading to better academic outcomes than those predicted merely by their previous accomplishments. A systematic review of other studies on student self-efficacy also confirmed a relationship between a student's belief in their capabilities and their academic performance.[49] This relationship transcends mere positive thinking; it fundamentally involves students' ability to exert control over their educational processes and shape their own academic experiences. By managing their learning and overcoming challenges, students not only foster greater self-efficacy but also enhance their overall educational success.

Additional research has shown that TL behaviors of school administration have a positive impact on teacher self-efficacy as teachers emulate the leadership qualities of their administrators.[50] Similarly, the actions and behaviors of teachers can affect the self-efficacy of their students. Teachers who exhibit supportive, encouraging, and transformational behaviors can significantly elevate their students' belief in their own abilities. For example, a science teacher who actively involves students in experiments and praises their investigative skills can boost confidence in their scientific capabilities. Similarly, a language arts teacher who provides constructive feedback and encourages creative expression can enhance students' self-efficacy in writing and critical thinking. Additionally, a sports coach who focuses on skill development rather than just winning can help athletes believe more in their physical abilities. These examples underscore the powerful role teachers play in shaping not just educational outcomes but the self-confidence with which students approach all aspects of their learning.

> ## Meet Marvin
>
> Marvin's high school experience was unfolding passively; he found himself in routine classes, viewing academics as merely a hurdle to clear on his way to basketball practice, which was his true passion. His indifferent attitude toward schoolwork was reflected in his disdain for honors or advanced placement courses, which he deemed unnecessary labor for no tangible benefit. His mantra to his mother was simple: "Mom, I'm never gonna use any of this stuff, anyway."
>
> Basketball, however, was where Marvin's heart lay. After quickly advancing from the freshman team to junior varsity, he was eyeing a spot on the varsity team. His dedication was evident as he and his neighbor Teddy practiced 50 free throws daily after school, the winner earning the right to ride shotgun the following day. He was also mindful of his health, adhering to a disciplined regimen of early nights and nutritious meals to optimize his performance.
>
> Everything changed when Marvin stepped into his freshman Spanish class, led by Ms. Garcia, whose passion for the language and its cultures

Meet Marvin (continued)

was infectious. Her dynamic teaching style, which included virtual tours of Spanish-speaking locales and interactive class discussions, captivated Marvin. For the first time, schoolwork resonated with him, and he excelled, surprising himself with straight As.

Ms. Garcia recognized Marvin's newfound enthusiasm and skill, suggesting he enroll in Honors Spanish the following year. Despite initial reservations about the increased workload, encouragement from his peers and the belief Ms. Garcia had in him pushed Marvin to accept the challenge. When he expressed his desire to advance to Mrs. Saggert, the guidance counselor, she promptly confirmed his eligibility, bolstered by Ms. Garcia's strong recommendation.

As Marvin's academic confidence grew, he joined the Spanish Club and learned about an upcoming trip to Puerto Rico. Excited about the opportunity to use his Spanish skills in a real-world context, he was initially concerned about the cost. He confided in Mrs. Saggert about his financial worries, and she helped him navigate the process of obtaining a scholarship,

Meet Marvin (continued)

ensuring he could attend the trip without burdening his family financially.

Marvin's journey through high school marked a profound transformation, ignited by his exposure to the Spanish language and culture, which expanded his horizons beyond the basketball court. He attended the trip to Puerto Rico, a pivotal experience that reinforced his appreciation for cultural diversity and education. Marvin's academic achievements didn't stop in high school; he went on to become the first person in his family to attend and graduate from college, turning his once narrow path into a broad avenue of possibilities.

Mrs. Saggert played a crucial role in reinforcing Marvin's self-efficacy, guiding him through moments of doubt and decision with unwavering support. Her assistance in securing a scholarship for the Puerto Rico trip was more than just financial aid; it was a profound affirmation of Marvin's capabilities and potential. This pivotal interaction not only alleviated his immediate concerns but also bolstered his belief in his ability to overcome challenges and achieve his goals. Mrs. Saggert's encouragement and recognition

> ### Meet Marvin (continued)
>
> helped transform Marvin's self-perception from one of a reluctant student to a confident achiever, illustrating the powerful impact of supportive educators on a student's journey toward self-discovery and success.

Client Testimonials

TLC is a wonderful environment for students who did not do well traditionally in their home district. They pinpoint the skills the students need to learn and facilitate individual growth. As a former administrator, I would have no problem recommending this school to others. I truly believe that not every child is made for every building. This is a great building for students to gain their confidence and feel successful.

—TLC Partner Organization

TLC was generous and gave my daughter the chance she needed to succeed. She suffered from severe depression and anxiety and could not handle the regular public school system. She was out more days than she was in and was in jeopardy of having to retake a year of school when we discovered TLC. The school's kind teachers were top notch.

Their counselors were terrific! This place allowed my daughter the independence she needed to grow in school without judgment. She did so well that she got a scholarship for college. During her time at TLC, she gained the confidence to become an EMT and is now getting her degree in emergency medicine! I cannot thank TLC and its kind staff enough! And I cannot praise the staff at this school enough for making a massive difference in so many young lives!

—PARENT, TLC LEADERSHIP ACADEMY

Our relationship with The Lincoln Center continues to grow year after year. They truly are a great nonprofit! We are happy to be a part of their continued growth in the community, as they expand and upgrade their facilities to serve today's youth. Their team truly cares and is *devoted to empowering the youth of today to be all they can be, and then some.* No doubt they will continue to succeed for years to come.

—TLC PARTNER ORGANIZATION

3.3 Socio-Emotional Well-Being

The third component of the student wellness construct, socio-emotional well-being, is essential for students' ability to manage their emotions and foster healthy relationships, which are crucial for their overall health and academic success. This element encompasses students' efforts to initiate and nurture interactions, thereby forming meaningful connections with peers, school staff, family, and friends. Socio-emotional well-being involves a student's self-esteem, trust in others, emotional intelligence, and commitment to active participation in life. In educational settings, socio-emotional skills are vital as they help students develop key competencies such as teamwork and collaboration, following directions, self-discipline, and attentiveness. Furthermore, the development of socio-emotional health is marked by the cultivation of trust, confidence, friendship, affection, and humor, enhancing the educational experience and personal growth.

Socio-emotional well-being is foundational in establishing a supportive and secure environment for students, influencing a variety of positive outcomes. A comprehensive review of over 200 school-based studies demonstrated that initiatives aimed at enhancing socio-emotional skills and overall well-being are linked to better attitudes, behaviors, and academic performance.[51] These improvements in attitudes and behaviors have a lasting impact; research has shown that socio-emotional skill development can significantly enhance mental health outcomes for students, even well beyond the duration of the interventions.[52] Additionally, another set of researchers identified that aspects of socio-emotional well-being are strong predictors of outcomes such as self-efficacy, perseverance, peer support, and empathy, among others.[53]

The initiatives to evaluate socio-emotional skills primarily involved educational interventions, highlighting that socio-emotional well-being can be developed through structured learning. These studies indicated that teacher support for student achievement, nurturing teacher-student relationships that foster connectedness, cooperative learning, and positive classroom environments are crucial in cultivating these skills. The evidence from these studies reinforces our confidence in the TE model, which integrates socio-emotional well-being, linking teacher behaviors with student outcomes, and forms a core part of our holistic approach to TE.

Client Testimonials

We adopted our son from a Russian orphanage when he was almost ten years old. He had a tough start in life. His high school years were also very challenging in many ways. He attended three different schools for parts of the ninth, tenth, and eleventh grades (lots of drama) and dropped out of school for a year. He experienced healing at a rehab place and returned to our town at age 20. We enrolled him at our local public school, which placed him part-time into TLC's Leadership Academy. He began to believe in people again. That year was life-changing for our son. It gave him hope for his future. The principal and staff of TLC were a fantastic support to our son! He began to take an interest in life. They educated and encouraged him in many ways through his graduation from high school. They also awarded him a college scholarship. We were so proud of him and grateful to TLC for their strong support.

—PARENTS, TLC LEADERSHIP ACADEMY

TLC has an open-concept layout, which my son loves. He was always a victim of bullying that was "never seen" happening! TLC was not one of the approved private schools contracted with our district at that time, but we insisted he go there! Upon the school district visiting the school and learning what TLC has to offer students, they signed a contract. My son has been going to TLC's Leadership Academy for almost four years. He now goes to school every day without a fight. He makes friends with teachers and students. He knows and believes that they genuinely care about him. His grades went from Ds and Fs to As! He has been able to reduce his medications and has not needed nearly as much outpatient therapy as before going to TLC. His future seems much brighter now. We have peace in our home again. Our son can talk about his traumatic past instead of harboring it. He enjoys going to school now and has friends and teachers who "get it"! He is finally happy and has hope once again! And so do I! Thank you, thank you, TLC!

—Parent, TLC Leadership Academy

Meet Allie

Gusts of wind chill the University of West Chester's campus on a winter morning, but the dorms provide a cozy spot away from the rawness of the weather. Inside one of these dorms sits a smiling Allie, a first-year student at WCU and former student of The Lincoln Center's Leadership Academy. Allie has dealt with mental illness almost her entire life, but you wouldn't know it today.

Yet, during her first year at the Academy, Allie felt suspicious of the staff and stayed withdrawn from her peers. She routinely slept on a couch at school to avoid going to class. Allie's therapists initially thought she struggled with borderline personality disorder, causing school-avoidant tendencies.

Meet Allie (continued)

Next, she went to even greater lengths to avoid school. She pretended to faint. Allie's case manager referred to this "ailment" as "fainting goat syndrome" because Allie would keel over like some goats with a genetic mutation that causes them to faint when frightened. Allie tested the boundaries, seeing how far she could push the "fainting goat" act and began pretending to faint at The Academy to avoid class. The school was required by law to call an ambulance! The fainting goat phase lasted months.

A third and final ruse to avoid school was when Allie and a friend planned and executed a fake fight. The end game was to get suspended from school so they could not attend class.

Sleeping, fainting, and fighting.

However, things started to change at The Lincoln Center during Allie's second year. She began putting effort into classes and understood that the people in her school environment wanted to help her be happy and productive. She believed in them and started trusting The Lincoln Center staff.

Allie formed relationships and grew invested in the people around her. "Allie's bubbly personality and positivity will always stand out when I

Meet Allie (continued)

think of her," says Rebecca, Lead Counselor at the Leadership Academy. "Allie could have had a rough day but would always check in before she left to say goodbye and did so with a smile. She wants the best for those around her."

Soon, Allie had the confidence to attend the Technical College High School part-time for their animal science program and became a certified animal care assistant. Unfortunately, though Allie has a great love for animals, she's allergic to almost everything! Therefore, she is now pursuing a degree in social work. And after her first semester at West Chester University, Allie's GPA earned her a spot on the dean's list.

Allie has adjusted exceptionally well to campus life. "Sometimes the social stuff gets to be a bit much," said Allie. But overall, she's been excelling in the classroom and thriving on campus. "I'm attending weekly therapy and functioning well with that," said Allie. "I'm off all my medications, which no one ever thought would be a thing."

Other people are excited, too. Kerri, Chief Program Officer at The Lincoln Center for Family and Youth and a person who knows Allie well, said, "It's impressive how Allie has learned to manage

Meet Allie (continued)

her mental health through connecting with others and engaging in her treatment. She has found many positive outlets, but it's through her self-efficacy that she has a more positive sense of self which, has allowed her to manage so well."

If she needs a break, Allie copes by listening to music, writing, and playing with fidget cubes. "I can safely say I'm in a stable place, and I know I am getting to a place where I will be able to succeed in social work. Life is going well. Things are going right."

—Excerpt from "From Fainting to Flying: A Short Story"
(https://TheLincolnCenter.com/blog)

Chapter 4

Student Performance: The Wave

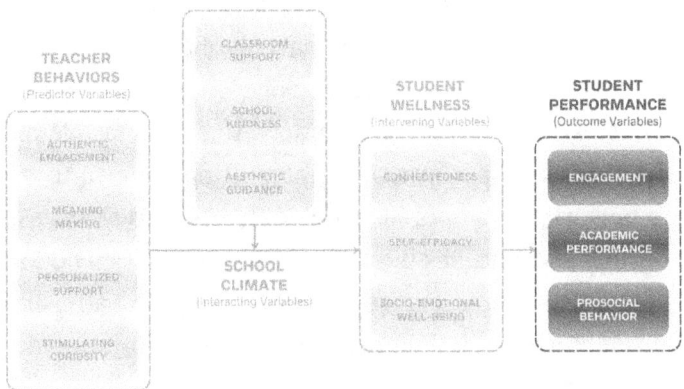

The ultimate aim of the Transformational Education (TE) model is to enhance student performance, a goal that is built upon the foundation of transformational teacher behaviors, a supportive school climate, and overall student wellness. This comprehensive approach is designed to not only elevate academic performance but also boost student engagement and encourage prosocial behaviors, creating a holistic educational experience.

In the field of education, traditional metrics like course grades and standardized test scores have long dominated the measures of student performance. However, a shift has been occurring as some educators advocate for a broader interpretation of performance that encompasses student transformation and growth. This expanded perspective emphasizes character building and community engagement, highlighting qualities such as empathy, kindness, cooperation, and understanding. The TE model embraces these nonacademic dimensions of performance, integrating them into its framework. This approach not only measures success through these values but also reinforces the conviction that skills such as engaging, connecting, empathizing, and demonstrating kindness are essential for students to lead healthy, productive lives.

4.1 Engagement

Engagement is the first TE component of student performance. It is defined by how deeply a student participates in and connects with the process of meaningful learning.[54] Engagement can manifest in various productive activities that facilitate educational advancement, such as a student's motivation to complete homework or their active participation in classroom activities. Additionally, engagement includes a student's ability to self-monitor their understanding and effectively communicate their learning progress. Another aspect of engagement is the student's adherence to instructions and their clear intention to learn. Universally, educators regard engagement as a highly valued and positive outcome of effective teaching strategies.

Furthermore, engagement is a strong predictor of enhanced student performance in various areas. It's not surprising that studies have connected high levels of student engagement with Transformational Leadership (TL) at the school level.[55] Given this correlation, it is logical to anticipate that both transformational school leadership and teacher leadership will boost student engagement, thereby improving overall student performance outcomes. After all, enhancing student success is the fundamental goal of education.

Meet Kerri

Kerri saw an ad in a church bulletin for a job as a resident aide in a nearby group home for intellectually and physically challenged individuals. At 16, Kerri knew this was for her.

She worked at the group home throughout high school. As she looked toward college, she wanted to focus her education on this population. The school

Meet Kerri (continued)

counselors helped her apply to college programs for special education because that is the best major for those who want to work with the special-needs population.

Kerri began as an elementary and special education dual major, but to her surprise, she didn't like it. She didn't feel at home or energized by the courses. So Kerri dropped the elementary education portion of the major and stuck with special education. She continued to struggle. She felt she'd made a mistake and didn't want to be a teacher.

The time came for a regularly scheduled meeting with Mr. Crouse, the college advisor. He genuinely listened as Kerri described her life goals. She talked about her dislike of putting together a mixed-media bulletin board for a classroom and many other reasons she currently felt misplaced. Mr. Crouse was attentive to all the details of her situation. Kerri was definitely engaged in her education, enough to know it was uncomfortable and leading her to a place she didn't want to go. Her reasons were valid and self-reflective. Mr. Crouse finally asked, "Have you ever heard about or considered the field of social work?"

Meet Kerri (continued)

Social work? No. Kerri reiterated that she wanted to work with special-needs individuals and families.

Mr. Crouse explained that it was all possible and then some; he described the social work field and degree. Kerri was intrigued, and that curiosity sparked a pivotal moment in her life. Becoming a social work major would open doors that Kerri did not even know existed. Mr. Crouse went even further; he tailored Kerri's junior-year schedule to meet the program's needs. This enabled her to graduate on time despite changing majors late in college.

Mr. Crouse had become a real mentor for her, and Kerri followed his advice to pursue a master's degree in social work and to license right away. Kerri's engagement in her education, alongside Mr. Crouse's guidance, impacted her future! As a result, Kerri was able to fulfill her goal of working with special-needs populations in the field of disabilities, but she also went on to a long career in child welfare, community counseling, and education . . . all as a social worker with a passion for at-risk populations.

Client Testimonials

I wouldn't have graduated high school if it weren't for TLC. The school allowed me to tune in to my education and eventually graduate. That positioned me to attend and graduate from the trade school I had always dreamed of attending. I am now working in my chosen field. I am experiencing great success in my life due to the help and education I received while attending TLC.

—Graduate, TLC Leadership Academy

After graduating from TLC, I completed my associate's degree from community college and am now working toward my bachelor's degree at Wilmington University. My teachers and the staff at TLC had a lot of patience with me when I was a student that led me to all the success I have today. Thanks to everyone who supported me.

—Graduate, TLC Leadership Academy

4.2 Academic Performance

Academic performance in school settings has traditionally been quantified through course grades and standardized test scores. Within the TE model, however, academic performance encompasses more than these metrics; it includes demonstrated skills and proficiency in written assignments, the academic rigor of the work, and the durability of learning. This implies not only the retention of knowledge but also the long-term utility and maintenance of acquired skills. The link between school leadership and student academic achievement is well-established and extensively documented in educational research.[56] However, and unfortunately, there is limited research on the impact of the teacher-student relationship on academic performance, although some studies have been conducted. For example, one study showed that effective instruction is marked by a teacher's genuine engagement with students and their support in the learning process.[57] Yet there continue to be relatively few studies that delve into how teacher behaviors and the overall learning environment contribute to student achievement.[58]

Reflecting on the established connection between school leadership and student academic achievement as outlined in the TE model, it's clear that expanding the metrics of academic performance enriches our understanding of student success. This model not only acknowledges traditional indicators such as grades and test scores but also emphasizes the critical role of demonstrated skills and the long-term utility of learning. Moreover, while research into the impact of the teacher-student relationship remains limited, the existing studies underscore the effectiveness of teacher behaviors like genuine engagement and supportive interaction. This supports the TE model's assertion that teacher behaviors such as authentic engagement, meaning making, personalized support, and stimulating curiosity are vital for enhancing academic outcomes. These findings reinforce the necessity of fostering an educational environment where teachers are actively involved in shaping the learning experience to meet the diverse needs of students, as vividly demonstrated by our experiences at The Lincoln Center. This approach not only boosts academic performance but also aligns with the broader objectives of TE and TL.

Client Testimonials

TLC is an amazing school. In high school, the teachers prepared and helped me get my grades up so I could graduate with my class. They're patient, compassionate, and, most of all, determined to see each and every one succeed.

—Graduate, TLC Leadership Academy

I have made connections at TLC that have stayed with me for years after graduating. Recently, I earned a bachelor's degree in finance and management information systems at Temple University's Fox School of Business after completing my senior year of high school at TLC. I was fortunate enough to be offered an opportunity at Vanguard to work as a brokerage investment professional and personal investor associate. After beginning my career roughly six months ago, I cannot sufficiently express my appreciation for TLC. On top of the phenomenal staff and program they offer, they also provide scholarship awards available to those pursuing continuing education beyond high school. I was fortunate enough to be one of those students selected to receive this aid. If it were not for TLC's devotion and support to their students, I would not be in the wonderful situation I am in today. For that, I thank TLC.

—Graduate, TLC Leadership Academy

TLC impacted my life in many ways. Academically, because all of the teachers, staff, and administration helped me graduate and continue to achieve my goals while staying focused to strive to get to where I wanted to go—to get into a four-year HBCU college. I'm so thankful to everyone at TLC for all they have done for me.

—Graduate, TLC Leadership Academy

4.3 Prosocial Behaviors

Within the framework of TE, student performance encompasses much more than mere academic metrics. A student's capacity for empathy and the demonstration of kindness are equally important outcomes. These qualities, often overlooked in conventional teaching and learning models, are increasingly recognized in contemporary educational approaches as vital markers of success both in education and in life more generally.[59] Thankfully, there is an increasing recognition that social and emotional learning matters. At The Lincoln Center, we categorize empathy and kindness as key socio-emotional behaviors, which together signal student success. Collectively, we refer to these important qualities as prosocial behaviors.

The concept of prosocial behaviors first emerged in the 1970s within the social sciences, originally developed as a counterpoint to antisocial behaviors. Generally, prosocial behaviors are defined as actions demonstrating a concern for the welfare, feelings, and rights of others. Such behaviors typically include acts of helping, comforting, collaborating, and sharing. From this wide spectrum of behaviors, TE emphasizes empathy and kindness. Empathy primarily involves an internal process of understanding others' emotions, which enables effective emotional communication.[60] Conversely, kindness is externally focused and involves actions that positively impact the lives of others,[61] encompassing behaviors such as respecting teachers, sharing with those in need, fulfilling promises, and offering comfort to those distressed.[62]

Educational researchers widely acknowledge that teachers play a significant role in cultivating empathy and kindness among students.[63] Studies in school environments where teachers embody the principles of the

TE model—authentic engagement, meaning making, personalized support, and stimulating curiosity—have shown promising outcomes. Observations in such settings reveal that students not only engage in empathetic and kind interactions with one another but also exhibit altruism, acceptance of diverse groups, and an intrinsic motivation to act positively.[64]

These findings are heartening for us at The Lincoln Center as we advocate for TE. This educational approach not only aligns with our values but has also demonstrated its efficacy in fostering essential and beneficial outcomes like prosocial behaviors. It underscores our belief in TE as a transformative educational model that prepares students not just for academic success but for life as compassionate, engaged citizens.

Client Testimonials

I've been getting help from TLC for a while. The school is home to some of the most amazing people I know. I have a therapist there at school, and she is amazing! She's very kind, empathetic, and understanding. The teachers at TLC never pressure me to say something I don't want to. At first, I was scared and nervous to open up and talk to someone, but after a couple of weeks, I started opening up and couldn't feel better! This is a good recommendation because not only do you get the help you need, they care. They will do anything they can to help you.

This makes me want to help others, too. In only a couple of months, I've been feeling better. So, it's safe to say this is a pretty good organization.

—STUDENT, TLC LEADERSHIP ACADEMY

I came across TLC when searching for help for my son, who was suffering from anxiety and depression. He was refusing to go to school, and the medicines and therapies were not helping. My son needed a therapeutic school that could put his mental well-being first and academics second. Most of the alternative schools in our area are for students with behavior issues. Being surrounded by negative behaviors from his peers only made things worse for him, so I knew these other schools would not help him. I found TLC's Leadership Academy after doing lots of research on the web. We made an appointment to visit the school and immediately knew it was the right fit for him! It was the first time I saw hope in my son's eyes in years!

—PARENT, TLC LEADERSHIP ACADEMY

STUDENT PERFORMANCE | THE WAVE

Meet Sara

I was in my twenties and had been working my first "grown-up" job for six years. It felt comfortable; the people were friendly, and I enjoyed the work. The job was in my hometown, close to what I had always known—predictable and safe. By nature, I seldom took risks. Yet I wondered, was there more out there for me?

In a brave moment, I applied for a job in another town. I am not sure what I expected, but I was afraid of the unknown and excited about what could be.

Soon after, I got a phone call from Shannon late on a weeknight. She was setting up interviews for the job and wanted the company to consider me for the position. But there was work to do on my application, so she asked whether I had the time to keep talking. Yes.

Later that same evening, we wrapped up our phone call. For nearly two hours, Shannon had put me through the wringer. She made a zillion recommendations to improve my résumé and coached me on interview questions.

When I got off the phone, I felt defeated and inexperienced. She ripped my résumé apart and hated my answers to the interview questions. There's no way I'd get this job!

> ## *Meet Sara (continued)*
>
> *I was drained but intrigued and invigorated, maybe even excited about the next steps. I was eager to follow Shannon's advice and take a chance. Shannon gave me personalized support and stimulated my curiosity through her mentorship. I had no idea how this would affect my life!*
>
> *I had one more meeting with Shannon before my interview. I got the job! The new position was challenging and exposed me to much more than my previous role. These experiences proved invaluable to my growth in my field and personal development. Shannon's brief mentorship and phone call were pivotal moments in my life.*
>
> *Seventeen years later, Shannon and I are still in touch. I will always regard Shannon as a mentor who changed the trajectory of my life's path with one unexpected phone call. This one moment mattered. It is an example of how the butterfly effect rerouted my path and impacted my life in remarkable ways.*

I'll conclude this section of the book with a personal story that sparked a chain of events, ultimately inspiring the creation of the TE model. In 2006, I was well into my tenure at Wachovia Bank in Charlotte, North Carolina, when I attended a project kickoff meeting with a dozen strangers. During introductions, one person, Pat, caught my attention with his intentional language and heartfelt mention of his family. He explained that he and his wife, already parents to three biological children, had recently adopted three more—two from Africa and one from China. His story was intriguing and inspiring.

Pat's personal calling and passion for helping the "least of these" resonated with me. After the meeting, I reintroduced myself and suggested we meet for lunch, which sparked a lifelong friendship. It was through Pat that I first learned about Regent University, a private Christian school in Virginia Beach, where he had completed his graduate studies. Although I had considered pursuing my doctorate later in life, his story reignited my interest in academia sooner than planned.

While my educational aspirations started with Mr. Sellers in the eighth grade of middle school and continued with Tony's encouragement to obtain my MBA, my formal education journey, in a sense, ended with Pat. Following the 2008 economic downturn, I decided to leave corporate America, pursue a PhD at Regent University, and shift my career to academia and nonprofit work.

Completing my doctoral studies in 2014, this educational journey not only altered my professional path but also transformed my worldview. While my engineering and MBA studies had presented problems with clear-cut answers, my PhD program introduced me to a new world, the social and behavioral sciences, where solutions are nuanced and context-dependent. This educational experience was transformative, teaching me that addressing social issues is as much an art as it is a science. I am grateful to Pat for setting me on this path with his powerful story of family and purpose. His example not only sparked an interest in furthering my formal education but also created a ripple that led to a fulfilling new career and equipped me with a richer perspective on life's complexities. This deeper understanding of the intricacies of human behavior and social interactions directly informed the development of the multivariate TE model.

Summary and Call to Action

The TE model proposes that certain teacher leadership behaviors in the classroom, coupled with a supportive school-wide culture, can have a significant and positive impact on student outcomes. This model is the product of extensive research and has been carefully integrated into the educational interventions we provide at The Lincoln Center for Family and Youth. In addition to the theoretical underpinnings rooted in research, the stories and testimonials included in this book also provide anecdotal support for the effectiveness of TE. Teaching practices that align with TE principles and are bolstered by a kind, supportive, and aesthetically stimulating environment can boost student wellness and academic performance. Scholarly research provides support for four crucial TE teacher behaviors: engaging authentically with students, fostering dialogue that explores meaning and purpose, providing customized and personalized support, and promoting intellectual curiosity.

Improving education in communities, especially those that are underserved, is a complex and nuanced endeavor that requires thoughtful and tailored approaches. Student engagement and performance are influenced by a multitude of factors, making it insufficient to assess from just one perspective. TE provides a multidimensional approach and is based on the principles of TL and substantial evidence linking TE teacher behaviors with outcomes at both the student and school levels. It elucidates how teacher actions, moderated by school climate and mediated by student wellness, directly and indirectly impact student performance. My hope is to inspire and equip educators everywhere to embrace and implement this transformative approach.

School administrators are encouraged to adopt the TE model to improve not only student outcomes but also teacher development. TE, which highlights the pivotal leadership role that teachers play in their classrooms, can also inform and enhance the process for evaluating teacher performance. Traditional evaluation tools often fall short in fostering ongoing development. However, a more refined evaluation approach can promote continuous professional growth by offering teachers targeted guidance to further their skills and effectiveness.[65] These interventions have proven effective in my own experience, revitalizing educational settings for the benefit of our children and youth, preparing future leaders to profoundly change lives, communities, and the world—the ultimate goal of education.

Thank you for joining me in exploring the TE model. I invite you to consider how this approach could positively impact your school and students.

For educators seeking to implement these principles in their schools and classrooms, the companion book—*An Application Guide to Transformational Education*—provides self-assessments, case studies, and lesson-planning activities

Appendix A: Glossary of Terms

Transformational Leadership (TL) A model designed to effect change via the leadership's persuasive power, characterized by four core practices: embodying role model qualities (idealized influence), providing motivational encouragement (inspirational motivation), attending to the individual needs of followers (individual consideration), and fostering innovation and critical thinking (intellectual stimulation).

Transformational Education (TE) A pedagogical model that views teachers as leaders, describing the relationships among teacher behaviors, school climate, student wellness, and performance outcomes. Central to the model are four core teacher behaviors: fostering genuine connections between educators and students (authentic engagement), encouraging learners to find purpose and value in their studies (meaning making), providing tailored support to meet individual needs (personalized support), and nurturing a deep sense of inquiry and exploration (stimulating curiosity).

Teacher Behaviors

Authentic Engagement Teachers demonstrate the value of every student by connecting with genuine care and without judgment, modeling healthy interaction in a safe space.

Meaning Making Teachers believe each life is significant and seek to help each student find meaning in their choices, appreciate their progress, and become intentional in their identified purpose.

Personalized Support Teachers adjust their approach to the needs, goals, and strengths of each student they serve, so every student feels safe and able to grow, learn, and heal.

Stimulating Curiosity Teachers empower students to become more connected to the world around them, challenging them to think about and solve problems in new ways while encouraging curiosity about themselves and others.

School Climate

Classroom Support The empathetic and caring behaviors exhibited by the school toward the classroom environment; this empathy and care can flow toward students from teachers, staff, and other students.

School Kindness Voluntary, intentional behaviors that are helpful and beneficial to another person.

Aesthetic Guidance The efforts made to create favorable aesthetic experiences that improve the students' experience in the classroom.

Student Wellness

Connectedness The extent to which students feel part of the community within their school context, family, and friends.

Self-Efficacy The degree to which students sense the power to make choices that affect themselves and their larger contexts.

Socio-Emotional Well-Being Students' initiation, cultivation, and response to others that move them to form relationships with peers, school staff, parents, relatives, and friends.

Student Performance

Academic Performance Demonstrated skill and proficiency in written work, academic quality, and durability of learning.

Engagement The degree to which a student is involved and immersed in the work of meaningful learning.

Prosocial Behaviors Students' ability to empathize and enact kindness.

Appendix B: Endnotes

Introduction to Transformational Education

1. T. Coladarci, "Teachers' Sense of Efficacy and Commitment to Teaching," *Experimental Education* 60, no. 4 (2002): 323–37.

2. K. Leithwood, "The Move toward Transformational Leadership," *Educational Leadership* 49 (1992): 8–12.

3. B. Bass, "Leadership: Good, Better, Best," *Organizational Dynamics* 13 (1985): 26–40, https://doi.org/10.1016/0090-2616(85)90028-2.

   B. Bass and B. Avolio, *Improving Organizational Effectiveness through Transformational Leadership* (Thousand Oaks, CA: Sage, 1994).

K. Leithwood and D. Jantzi, "Transformational School Leadership for Large-Scale Reform: Effects on Students, Teachers, and Their Classroom Practices," *School Effectiveness and School Improvement* 17, no. 2 (2006): 201–27.

4. K. Leithwood, "The Move toward Transformational Leadership," *Educational Leadership* 49 (1992): 8–12.

5. B. Bass, "Leadership: Good, Better, Best," *Organizational Dynamics* 13 (1985): 26–40, https://doi.org/10.1016/0090-2616(85)90028-2.

6. K. Leithwood and D. Jantzi, "Explaining Variation in Teachers' Perceptions of Principals' Leadership: A Replication," *Journal of Educational Administration* 35, no. 4 (1997): 312–31.

K. Leithwood and D. Jantzi, "Transformational School Leadership Effects: A Replication," *School Effectiveness and School Improvement* 10, no. 4 (1999): 451–79.

K. Leithwood and J. Sun, "The Nature and Effects of Transformational School Leadership: A Meta-analytic Review of Unpublished Research," *Educational Administration Quarterly* 48, no. 3 (2012): 387–423.

7. J. Pounder, "Transformational Leadership: Practicing What We Teach in the Management Classroom," *Journal of Education for Business* 84, no. 1 (2010): 2–6, https://doi.org/10.3200/JOEB.84.1.2-6.

   J. Pounder, "Quality Teaching through Transformational Classroom Leadership," *Quality Assurance in Education* 22, no. 3 (2014): 273–85, https://doi.org/10.1108/QAE-12-2013-0048.

8. V. Battistich, D. Solomon, M. Watson, and E. Schaps, "Caring School Communities," *Educational Psychologist* 32 (1997): 137–51.

9. G. T. Freeman, J. Blackstone, and M. J. Burchard, "A Proposed Model for Transformational Education," *Education Leadership Review* 21, no. 1 (2020): 255–72.

Chapter 1

10. L. K. Seashore, B. Dretzke, and K. Wahlstrom, "How Does Leadership Affect Student Achievement? Results from a National US Survey," *School Effectiveness and School Improvement* 21, no. 3 (2010): 315–36.

11. S. Boss and J. Larmer, *Project Based Teaching: How to Create Rigorous and Engaging Learning Experiences* (Alexandria, VA: ASCD, 2018).

12. V. Battistich, D. Solomon, M. Watson, and E. Schaps, "Caring School Communities," *Educational Psychologist* 32 (1997): 137–51.

13. S. Cetin, "An Analysis on the Qualities of School Life and Classroom Engagement Levels of Students," *South African Journal of Education* 38, no. 1 (2018): S1–S13.

14. H. Smith and S. Higgins, "Opening Classroom Interaction: The Importance of Feedback," *Cambridge Journal of Education* 36, no. 4: 485–502.

15. J. Sebastian, E. Allensworth, and H. Huang, "The Role of Teacher Leadership in How Principals Influence Classroom Instruction and Student Learning," *American Journal of Education* 123 (2016): 69–108.

16. J. Varney, "Leadership as Meaning Making," *Human Resource Management International Digest* 17, no. 5 (2009): 3–5, https://doi.org/10.1108/09670730910974251.

17. V. Battistich, D. Solomon, M. Watson, and E. Schaps, "Caring School Communities," *Educational Psychologist* 32 (1997): 137–51.

18. J. Varney, "Leadership as Meaning Making," *Human Resource Management International Digest* 17, no. 5 (2009): 3–5, https://doi.org/10.1108/09670730910974251.

19. M. Ibrahim, S. Ghavifekr, S. Ling, S. Siraj, and M. I. Azeez, "Can Transformational Leadership Influence Teachers' Commitment towards Organization, Teaching Profession, and Students Learning? A Quantitative Analysis," *Asia Pacific Education Review* 15 (2014): 177–90.

20. V. Battistich, D. Solomon, M. Watson, and E. Schaps, "Caring School Communities," *Educational Psychologist* 32 (1997): 137–51.

21. V. Battistich, D. Solomon, M. Watson, and E. Schaps, "Caring School Communities," *Educational Psychologist* 32 (1997): 137–51.

22. J. Sebastian, E. Allensworth, and H. Huang, "The Role of Teacher Leadership in How Principals Influence Classroom Instruction and Student Learning," *American Journal of Education* 123 (2016): 69–108.

23. A. Benner, A. Boyle, and F. Bakhtiari, "Understanding Students' Transition to High School: Demographic Variation and the Role of Supportive Relationships," *Journal of Youth and Adolescence* 46, no. 10 (2017): 2129–42, https://doi.org/10.1007/s10964-017-0716-2.

24. J. Tennant, M. Demaray, C. Malecki, M. Terry, M. Clary, and N. Elzinga, "Students' Ratings of Teacher Support and Academic and Social-Emotional Wellbeing," *School Psychology Quarterly* 30, no. 4 (2015): 494–512, https://doi.org/10.1037/spq0000106.

25. V. Battistich, D. Solomon, M. Watson, and E. Schaps, "Caring School Communities," *Educational Psychologist* 32 (1997): 137–51.

26. J. Crough, "Stimulating Curiosity in STEM Higher Education: Connecting Practices and Purposes through ePortfolios," in *Blended Learning Designs in STEM Higher Education*, ed. C. Allen, W. Shurety, and J. Crough (Singapore: Springer, 2019), 77–98.

    J. Lee, E. Law, D. Chun, and K. Chan, "Cultivating Self-Management and Leadership Skills among Hong Kong Students," *Curriculum and Teaching* 32, no. 1 (2017): 5–24; M. Lindholm, "Promoting Curiosity?" *Science and Education* 27, no. 9–10 (2018): 987–1002.

27. M. Lindholm, "Promoting Curiosity?" *Science and Education* 27, no. 9–10 (2018): 987–1002.

28. M. Ibrahim, S. Ghavifekr, S. Ling, S. Siraj, and I. M. Azeez, "Can Transformational Leadership Influence Teachers' Commitment towards Organization, Teaching Profession, and Students Learning? A Quantitative Analysis," *Asia Pacific Education Review* 15 (2014): 177–90.

29. M. Ibrahim, S. Ghavifekr, S. Ling, S. Siraj, and I. M. Azeez, "Can Transformational Leadership Influence Teachers' Commitment towards Organization, Teaching Profession, and Students Learning? A Quantitative Analysis," *Asia Pacific Education Review* 15 (2014): 177–90.

30. S. Bolkan and A. Goodboy, "Transformational Leadership in the Classroom: The Development and Validation of the Student Intellectual Stimulation Scale," *Communication Reports* 23 (2010): 91–105.

    S. Bolkan, A. Goodboy, and D. Griffin, "Teacher Leadership and Intellectual Stimulation: Improving Students' Approaches to Studying through Intrinsic Motivation," *Communication Research Reports* 28, no. 4 (2011): 337–46.

Chapter 2

31. J. Cohen, "Social, Emotional, Ethical, and Academic Education: Creating a Climate for Learning, Participation in Democracy, and Wellbeing," *Harvard Educational Review* 76 (2006): 201–37.

32. L. O'Brennan and C. Bradshaw, "Importance of School Climate," http://www.nea.org/.

33. J. Durlak, R. Weissberg, A. Dymnicki, R. Taylor, and K. Schellinger, "Enhancing Students' Social and Emotional Development Promotes Success in School: Results of a Meta-analysis," *Child Development* 82 (2011): 474–501.

34. A. Ross, G. Grenier, and F. Kros, *Creating the upside down Organization: Transforming Staff to Save Troubled Children* (Baltimore: Children's Guild, 2005).

    V. Battistich, D. Solomon, M. Watson, and E. Schaps, "Caring School Communities," *Educational Psychologist* 32 (1997): 137–51.

35. L. Lester and D. Cross, "The Relationship between School Climate and Mental and Emotional Wellbeing over the Transition from Primary to Secondary School," *Psychology of Wellbeing* 5, no. 9 (2015): 1–15, https://doi.org/10.1186/s13612-015-0037-8.

36. N. Eisenberg, *Altruistic Emotion, Cognition, and Behavior* (Hillsdale, NJ: Erlbaum, 1986).

37. J.-T. Binfet, A. Gadermann, and K. Schonert-Reichl, "Measuring Kindness at School: Psychometric Properties of a School Kindness Scale for Children and Adolescents," *Psychology in the Schools* 53, no. 2 (2016): 111–26.

38. C. Day, Q. Gu, and P. Sammons, "The Impact of Leadership on Student Outcomes: How Successful School Leaders Use Transformational and Instructional Strategies to Make a Difference," Educational Administration Quarterly 52, no. 2 (2016): 221–58.

    J. Datu and N. Park, "Perceived School Kindness and Academic Engagement: The Mediational Roles of Achievement Goal Orientations," *School Psychology International* 40, no. 5 (2019): 456–73, https://doi.org/10.1177/0143034319854474.

39. J.-T. Binfet, A. Gadermann, and K. Schonert-Reichl, "Measuring Kindness at School: Psychometric Properties of a School Kindness Scale for Children and Adolescents," *Psychology in the Schools* 53, no. 2 (2016): 111–26.

40. J.-T. Binfet, A. Gadermann, and K. Schonert-Reichl, "Measuring Kindness at School: Psychometric Properties of a School Kindness Scale for Children and Adolescents," *Psychology in the Schools* 53, no. 2 (2016): 111–26.

41. C. Day, Q. Gu, and P. Sammons, "The Impact of Leadership on Student Outcomes: How Successful School Leaders Use Transformational and Instructional Strategies to Make a Difference," Educational Administration Quarterly 52, no. 2 (2016): 221–58.

    J. Datu and N. Park, "Perceived School Kindness and Academic Engagement: The Mediational Roles of Achievement Goal Orientations," *School Psychology International* 40, no. 5 (2019): 456–73, https://doi.org/10.1177/0143034319854474.

42. H. Hansen, A. Ropo, and E. Sauer, "Aesthetic Leadership," *Leadership Quarterly* 18, no. 6 (2017): 544–60.

43. H.-S. Lin, Z.-R. Hong, and Y.-Y. Cheng, "The Interplay of Classroom Learning Environment and Inquiry-Based Activities," *International Journal of Science Education* 31, no. 8 (2009): 1013–24, https://doi.org/10.1080/09500690701799391;

Q. Suleman and I. Hussain, "Effects of Classroom Physical Environment on the Academic Achievement Scores of Secondary School Students in Kohat Division, Pakistan," *International Journal of Learning and Development* 4, no. 1 (2014): 71–82, https://doi.org/10.5296/ijld.v4il.5174.

44. H.-S. Lin, Z.-R. Hong, and Y.-Y. Cheng, "The Interplay of Classroom Learning Environment and Inquiry-Based Activities," *International Journal of Science Education* 31, no. 8 (2009): 1013–24, https://doi.org/10.1080/09500690701799391.

Q. Suleman and I. Hussain, "Effects of Classroom Physical Environment on the Academic Achievement Scores of Secondary School Students in Kohat Division, Pakistan," *International Journal of Learning and Development* 4, no. 1 (2014): 71–82, https://doi.org/10.5296/ijld.v4il.5174.

Chapter 3

45. K. King, R. Vidourek, B. Davis, and W. McClellan, "Increasing Self-Esteem and School Connectedness through a Multidimensional Mentoring Program," *Journal of School Health* 72, no. 7 (2002): 294–99.

46. D. Osher, E. Spier, K. Kendziora, and C. Cai, "Improving Academic Achievement through Improving School Climate and Student Connectedness," Paper presentation at the Annual Meeting for the American Educational Research Association, San Diego, 2009.

47. L. Lester and D. Cross, "The Relationship between School Climate and Mental and Emotional Wellbeing over the Transition from Primary to Secondary School," *Psychology of Wellbeing* 5, no. 9 (2015): 1–15, https://doi.org/10.1186/s13612-015-0037-8.

48. S. Cassidy, "Resilience Building in Students: The Role of Academic Self-Efficacy," *Frontiers in Psychology* 6 (2015): 1–14, https://doi.org/10.3389/fpsyg.2015.01781.

49. T. Honicke and J. Broadbent, "The Influence of Academic Self-Efficacy on Academic Performance: A Systematic Review," *Educational Research Review* 17 (2016): 63–84, https://doi.org/10.1016/j.edurev.2015.11.002.

50. V. Battistich, D. Solomon, M. Watson, and E. Schaps, "Caring School Communities," *Educational Psychologist* 32 (1997): 137–51.

51. J. Durlak, R. Weissberg, A. Dymnicki, R. Taylor, and K. Schellinger, "Enhancing Students' Social and Emotional Development Promotes Success in School: Results of a Meta-analysis," *Child Development* 82 (2011): 474–501.

52. J. D. Hawkins, R. Kosterman, R. Catalano, K. Hill, and R. Abbott, "Effects of a Social Development Intervention in Childhood 15 Years Later," *Archives of Pediatric and Adolescent Medicine* 162 (2008): 1133–41.

53. M. J. Furlong, S. You, T. Renshaw, D. Smith, and M. O'Malley, "Preliminary Development and Validation of the Social and Emotional Health Survey for Secondary School Students," *Social Indicators Research* 117, no. 3 (2014): 1011–32.

Chapter 4

54. G. DuPaul, M. Rapport, and L. Perriello, "Teacher Ratings of Academic Skills: The Development of the Academic Performance Rating Scale," *School Psychology Review* 20, no. 2 (1991): 284–300.

55. K. Leithwood and D. Jantzi, "Explaining Variation in Teachers' Perceptions of Principals' Leadership: A Replication," *Journal of Educational Administration* 35, no. 4 (1997): 312–31.

    K. Leithwood and D. Jantzi, "Transformational School Leadership Effects: A Replication," *School Effectiveness and School Improvement* 10, no. 4 (1999): 451–79.

56. J. E. Boberg and S. Bourgeois, "The Effects of Integrated Transformational Leadership on Achievement," *Journal of Educational Administration* 54, no. 3 (2016): 357–74.

    J. Sebastian, E. Allensworth, and H. Huang, "The Role of Teacher Leadership in How Principals Influence Classroom Instruction and Student Learning," *American Journal of Education* 123 (2016): 69–108.

    J. Sun and K. Leithwood, "Transformational School Leadership Effects on Student Achievement," *Leadership and Policy in Schools* 11, no. 4 (2012): 418–51, https://doi.org/10.1080/15700763.2012.681001.

57. V. Battistich, D. Solomon, M. Watson, and E. Schaps, "Caring School Communities," *Educational Psychologist* 32 (1997): 137–51.

58. J. Sebastian, E. Allensworth, and H. Huang, "The Role of Teacher Leadership in How Principals Influence Classroom Instruction and Student Learning," *American Journal of Education* 123 (2016): 69–108.

59. J.-T. Binfet, A. Gadermann, and K. Schonert-Reichl, "Measuring Kindness at School: Psychometric Properties of a School Kindness Scale for Children and Adolescents," *Psychology in the Schools* 53, no. 2 (2016): 111–26.

60. R. N. Spreng, M. McKinnon, R. Mar, and B. Levine, "The Toronto Empathy Questionnaire: Scale Development and Initial Validation of a Factor-Analytic Solution to Multiple Empathy Measures," *Journal of Personality Assessment* 9, no. 1 (2009): 62–71.

61. K. Layous, K. Nelson, E. Oberle, K. Schonert-Reichl, and S. Lyubomirsky, "Kindness Counts: Prompting Prosocial Behavior in Preadolescents Boosts Peer Acceptance and Wellbeing," *PLoS One* 7, no. 12 (2012): 1–3.

62. K. Layous, K. Nelson, E. Oberle, K. Schonert-Reichl, and S. Lyubomirsky, "Kindness Counts: Prompting Prosocial Behavior in Preadolescents Boosts Peer Acceptance and Wellbeing," *PLoS One* 7, no. 12 (2012): 1–3.

S. Lamborn, K. Fischer, and S. Pipp, "Constructive Criticism and Social Lies: A Developmental Sequence for Understanding Honesty and Kindness in Social Interactions," *Developmental Psychology* 30 (1994): 495–508.

V. Battistich, D. Solomon, M. Watson, and E. Schaps, "Caring School Communities," *Educational Psychologist* 32 (1997): 137–51.

63. N. Eisenberg, R. Fabes, and T. Spinrad, "Prosocial Development," in *Handbook of Child Psychology: Social, Emotional, and Personality Development*, ed. N. Eisenberg (Hoboken, NJ: Wiley, 2016), 646–718).

64. V. Battistich, D. Solomon, M. Watson, and E. Schaps, "Caring School Communities," *Educational Psychologist* 32 (1997): 137–51.

Summary of Transformational Education Model

65. A. N. Warren and N. A. Ward, "'It Didn't Make Me a Better Teacher': Inservice Teacher Constructions of Dilemmas in High-Stakes Teacher Evaluation," *School Effectiveness and School Improvement* 30, no. 4 (2019): 531–48, https://doi.org/10.1080/09243453.2019.16191.

S. Lillejord and K. Børte, "Trapped between Accountability and Professional Learning? School Leaders and Teacher Evaluation," *Professional Development in Education* 46, no. 2 (2020): 274–91, https://doi.org/10.1080/19415257.2019.1585384.

www.ingramcontent.com/pod-product-compliance
Lightning Source LLC
Chambersburg PA
CBHW072048290426
44110CB00014B/1600